SATISFYING
SALADS

Tomato, Prosciutto & Fresh Mozzarella, page 30

SATISFYING
SALADS

RODALE

Printed in the United States of America
Rodale Inc. makes every effort to use acid-free ♾, recycled paper ♻.

Cover photograph: Mitch Mandel
Cover recipe: Greek Beef Salad
Courtesy of Cattlemen's Beef Board and
National Cattlemen's Beef Association, page 70
Food stylist: Diane Vezza
Illustrations: Judy Newhouse

Editorial Produced by:
BETH ALLEN ASSOCIATES, INC.

President/Owner: Beth Allen
Art Production Director: Laura Smyth (smythtype)
Photo Researcher: Valerie Vogel
Culinary Consultant/Food Editor: Deborah Mintcheff
Recipe Editor: Carol Prager
Public Relations Consultants: Stephanie Avidon, Melissa Moritz
Nutritionist: Michele C. Fisher, Ph.D., R.D.

Library of Congress Cataloging-in-Publication Data

Satisfying salads.
        p.   cm.
     Includes index.
     ISBN-13 978–1–59486–170–3 hardcover
     ISBN-10 1–59486–170–6 hardcover
     1. Salads.   I. Rodale (Firm)
   TX740.S316   2005
   641.8'3—dc22   2004026494

2   4   6   8   10   9   7   5   3   1   hardcover

We inspire and enable people to improve their lives and the world around them

For more of our products visit **rodalestore.com** or call 800-848-4735

CONTENTS

INTRODUCTION

Much more than a wedge of iceberg

Time was, not so long ago, salad usually meant a wedge of iceberg lettuce with a big spoonful of Russian dressing dripping over the sides or a slice of tomato aspic with a dollop of mayonnaise. On Sundays and special occasions, perhaps Grandmother would make her famous frozen fruit salad with those tiny marshmallows or her red strawberry mold with the berries inside. But those always seemed more like dessert than salad.

Luckily, today salad is no longer relegated to just the salad course. There always seems to be something new at the greens market to throw into the salad bowl—from arugula to dandelion greens to shrimp to salmon. And it turns easily into "The Main Event" or often takes its place "Off to the Side," accompanying the main course. Even better, some new food technologies are helping to make salads even faster and easier than ever before. Here in *Satisfying Salads* we bring it all to you—in the same streamlined, time-saving way as in all The Quick Cook books.

Are you tired of the same old green salad? Then take a minute to brush up on the many greens in "Navigating the New Lettuce Bin" (page 11) and make a list of the ones you'd like to try. Perhaps start off with Mixed Baby Greens with Apple, Bacon & Stilton (page 30) for an unbeatably refreshing mix of flavors. Or the all-time favorite Quick Caesar Salad (page 27), quicker than you ever thought possible—just 15 minutes from start to finish, thanks to a bag of store-bought salad greens. Or pick up one of those convenient bags of greens with veggies tossed in to make the California Classic Salad with Roquefort Dressing (page 25), also in just 15 minutes.

Next, discover how simple and scrumptious a salad for supper can be. Enjoy a taste of New York City with the Waldorf Chicken Salad (page 53), dine as they do on the West Coast with a Classic California Cobb (page 54), or experience true Tex-Mex fare by serving the Easy Taco Salad (page 44)—all in 30 minutes or less, just like all Quick Cook recipes. But that's not all. Also included are many salad dressings you can shake up fast—from that Classic Honey-Mustard Dressing (page 133) to the new darling of them all, Balsamic Vinaigrette (page 130).

No salad book would be complete without some fabulous fruit salads. You'll find ones for summertime and fall too—plus favorite fruit combinations in the *Cook to Cook* section on page 119 to help you create your own imaginative fruit salads. There are also some of those shimmering molded fruit salads. There's a Light & Fruity Raspberry Mold (page 108) that'll make a spectacular entrance into any dinner party. But first you might want to read all about the *Microwave in Minutes* feature on page 111 to see how your microwave can help you melt gelatin fast and easy—plus the *Salad Basics* tips (page 109) on how to unmold that mold fast, easy, and perfect every time.

Begin exploring the world of sensational salads by turning the page to "Fast Salad Fixings." Take a moment to see how to turn your salads into decorative designer ones with ease. Find out about the many flavored oils and vinegars that add layers of flavor to the salad bowl. And when it comes to chopping, dicing, and slicing salad ingredients, do you know how a mezzaluna and a mandoline can cut down your prep time? (Read all about them on pages 14 and 15.) Then find out how to make croutons quickly and easily by flavoring the ready-made ones out of a package from the *Time Savers* feature on page 132.

For the speediest salads in this collection, look for the SuperQuick label, such as the one found next to the Avocado Garden Salad on page 29—it's ready to eat in 15 minutes flat! Just like all of the other Quick Cook books, you'll find handy-to-have *Salad Basics*, such as how much salad to plan on for the number of folks you're serving (page 27), and *On the Menu* ideas to help you round out a meal. Some evening, when you have a few free minutes, enjoy reading *Food Facts* to trace fruit salads throughout history in America (page 116).

We've teamed up with test kitchens and food professionals, plus cooking pros and food manufacturers all across the country, to bring you *Satisfying Salads*—including reliable tested recipes that come out perfect every time. And remember, there are many other books in The Quick Cook series that will be coming your way soon. Each one is designed with its own special collections of just what you want in today's cookbooks—fast yet great-tasting recipes, beautiful photographs, and many never-fail tips and techniques. So head into the kitchen right now and begin discovering the sensational world of salads today—so much more than that wedge of iceberg but just as good as any grandmother used to make.

Classic California Cobb, page 54

Fast Salad Fixings

Scrumptious salads often start with only two simple ingredients: the freshest greens and a flavorful vinaigrette. That's plenty . . . but of course there's so much more to the salad story. Start off by discovering the many new greens available at farmers' markets. Layer in the flavor with pepper- or herb-infused oils and wine or fruit vinegars. Top it off with homemade croutons, spiced just the way you like them, then move on to cutting out fixing time with a special slicing tool. Now get ready to try the recipes—from mostly greens to shimmering fruit salads to coleslaw sides. All in less than 30 minutes of fixing time, and all guaranteed to bring salads into favor, whatever the time of day, whatever the season.

SALADS—THEN AND NOW

Over the centuries, the definition of a salad has remained the same: one food or a mix of several bound by a dressing. Even though salads date back well before medieval times, little has changed. The word relates to the Latin *sal* (salt), then *salata* (salted things), later to the Old English as *sallet* or salad. Then as now, one of the first salads was indeed vegetables eaten with a dressing of salt, oil, or vinegar. By medieval times, salads were green leaves, sometimes with flowers, just like today. The 17th century in Europe ushered in the grand sallets, much like our contemporary composed entrée salads: often with slices of roasted capon in the center of a large platter surrounded by pickled mushrooms, pickled oysters, fruits (such as lemons and oranges), almonds, potatoes, and pease (peas), all drizzled with vinegar and oil.

Here in America, the 19th century brought some American classics, such as the famous Waldorf salad, slices of molded tomato aspic, or wedges of iceberg with the forever favorite heaping spoonful of Russian or Thousand Island dressing. Salads then as now were also often regarded as ways to use up leftovers; roast beef salads and chicken salads were favorites and still are. Pickling was and still is popular—from beets to cucumbers to onions. Coleslaws, brought over by the Dutch, were considered a delicious way to turn cabbage into a salad and are considered an American classic.

Early in the 20th century, Jell-O, with all its fruit-filled shimmering molded creations, transformed the salad course and moved it very close to dessert. And after World War II, Americans began traveling abroad, wanting greens back home just like they enjoyed overseas, such as mesclun from France, radicchio from Italy, and snow peas from China. More soon-to-be classics began arriving on the salad scene, including Cobb salad, Caesar salad, and that all-time favorite chef salad. As for the seasoning and flavoring of salads, fresh herbs became popular for sprinkling onto salads. Homemakers soon embraced the idea of drizzling salads with oils and vinegars flavored with spices, herbs, and fruits. Many of these classics, and new creations too, are what's inside these pages. It's salads through the centuries, still and always sensational, satisfying, and delicious.

SALAD—YOUR WAY!

All salads have one thing in common—harmony. That is, all the colors, flavors, and textures of each ingredient must complement all of the others to create a harmonious, scrumptious creation. They must work and blend together to

Salad Basics

NAVAGATING THE NEW LETTUCE BIN

Things have changed in the farmers' markets—as well as in the fruit and vegetable section of your neighborhoods. Just look what's beyond iceberg.

ARUGULA (ROCKET)—Dark green, slender, small leaves with a peppery, pungent, almost bitter taste. Often, arugula is used with other greens to zip up the salad bowl. The smaller the leaf, the milder the flavor.

BABY LETTUCES (GREEN OR RED BABY BIBB, BABY RED OAK, LOLA ROSA, PIRATE, RED SAILS)—They're just miniatures of their larger mature versions, are great for tossing into salad bowls for variety, and perfect to use in composed salads.

BUTTERHEAD LETTUCE (BIBB AND BOSTON)—Both heads of lettuce with buttery, delicate, mild flavor and tender leaves. Bibb is smaller, but they're both similar in flavor.

BELGIAN ENDIVE—Small, tight heads of creamy-white pointed leaves and either green, yellow, or even purple at the tips. Known for the slightly bitter flavor that it adds to the salad.

CURLY ENDIVE (FRISÉE)—Head of lettuce with frilly, curly, sharp leaves with a slightly bitter taste. Heads have dark green leaves on the outside, white leaves on the inside of the head.

ESCAROLE (BROAD LEAF ENDIVE)—Also part of the endive group, its head is medium-green in color and has slightly waxy, scalloped leaves with a slightly bitter strong flavor that stands up well to strong-flavored dressings.

"GREENS" (CHARD, COLLARD, DANDELION, MUSTARD)—When using these in the salad bowl, look for the younger greens, as they're milder in flavor and more tender.

LEAF LETTUCES (GREEN, RED, OAK LEAF)—These are known for their loose heads (actually they look more like bunches held together at their base) with tender, mild flavors. Perfect to mix with iceberg in the salad bowl as they add more flavor and deeper colors.

MÂCHE (LAMB'S LETTUCE OR FIELD LETTUCE)—Small leaves, from pale to dark green, with a slight spoon shape and a very mild flavor. Toss with only mild-flavored greens, such as Bibb lettuce, and use only a mild vinaigrette, so as not to overpower its delicate flavor.

MESCLUN (GOURMET SALAD MIX)—The very popular mix of young baby greens sold in many farmers' markets and gourmet stores. It often includes: arugula, chervil, dandelion, frisée, oak leaf, mâche, radicchio, and sorrel.

RADICCHIO—Looks similar to a small head of red cabbage with tender leaves and a slightly bitter flavor. When separated, these leaves form small cups that are ideal for holding a salad such as chicken salad or tuna salad.

ROMAINE (COS)—Nothing new with this lettuce except its long, dark green leaves occasionally come with a bit of red on the tips, which look nice in the salad bowl.

SORREL (SOURGRASS)—Leaves resemble spinach in its shape and dark green color, but are overall smaller and have a different flavor of sharp lemon, which makes the perfect green to use in seafood salads.

SPINACH—This forever popular green comes with smooth leaves, often a little rippled on the edges, with a rich flavor. Baby spinach is also perfect for salads, as it's even more tender and delicate in flavor.

WATERCRESS—Small, dark green leaves with a crisp, peppery bite. For the best cress, pick a bunch without any yellow leaves. Keep very cold and pull the leaves off of their stems just before using.

Asian Spinach Salad, page 23

Old Bay Coleslaw, page 89

Chicken and Wild Rice Salad, page 56

form a delicious whole. Here are some of the basic types of salads, based on their overall design and composition:

- Tossed Salads—By far the favorite of most folks. The possibilities for types of leafy vegetables are numerous . . . and not all green (see "Navigating the New Lettuce Bin" on page 11). They differ in color (from greenish white to yellow to deep purple), in texture (from tender to sturdy), and in flavor (from mild to peppery). Mix them up for color and flavor. Have fun with the extras: tiny grape tomatoes, yellow bell peppers, toasted pecans, crumbled bacon, and all kinds of fruits. Now a word about dressings: They should season and spice the salad as you like—but not drown out its flavor. Use just enough dressing to coat the leaves, otherwise you'll end up with wet and soggy salad greens.

- Bound Salads—The creative possibilities are especially endless with these salads, but they have one thing in common: Their ingredients are gently combined to form a mass. The binding ingredient can be a light vinaigrette, as in pasta salads, or a creamy mayonnaise, as in a seafood or an egg salad. Just be sure to cut all salad ingredients the same size: small enough to be easily eaten with a fork.

- Composed Salads (the Designer Touch!)—Elegant, appetizing, and just perfect for a dinner party. There are four basic components—each one layering on the color, flavor, and texture. Composed salads begin with a base, often a layer or mix of greens or the thinnest layer of cucumber or tomato slices. Add the body of the salad next, perhaps a leafy vegetable of contrasting color and texture or another complete salad such as your favorite fruit or chicken. Put on the garnish next. It can be as substantial as shrimp or as simple as a colorful pansy or slivered basil. Now finish it off with the dressing, right before serving. One way to keep the beautiful design is to use a pourable dressing, such as a vinaigrette, that you've transferred to a spray bottle. Then gently mist the salad with the dressing right before taking it to the table.

THE BIG DRESS-UP!

The ways to dress up a salad are many: from the simple three-to-one vinaigrette (that's 3 parts oil to 1 part vinegar emulsified with a heaping spoonful of mustard) to a classic mayonnaise and everything in between (turn to page 125 and check out the "Dress It Up!" chapter). Experiment to your heart's content with the many vinegars and oils on the market that have plenty of flavor, seasoning, and spice.

VINEGARS—red or white wine; balsamic, tarragon, or rosemary; fruits such as raspberry and blueberry or other.

OILS—spiced with pepper, garlic, or herbs.

IT'S IN THE BAG!

The bags of prewashed, premixed, pretorn greens and other vegetables are just made for The Quick Cook! And there always seems to be a different one to discover. Although they have all been washed before they come to you, it's still a good idea to rinse and spin dry them before using. When buying, check the "best if used by date" and pick the bag that looks the freshest (avoid any greens with brown edges). After bringing it home, store it in its bag in the refrigerator crisper drawer; if you use part of a bag, close it tightly (do not put into another bag). Most packages are bags of greens, some are classics like vegetable coleslaw, still others are a salad-in-a-bag such as Caesar, complete with dressing and croutons too; while others have that "organic" label. All go from bag to salad bowl within minutes. Here are a few that might catch your attention on your next shopping trip:

- American blend—iceberg, romaine, carrots, cabbage, and radishes
- European—romaine, iceberg, radicchio, endive, and other leafy lettuces
- Butter lettuces—tender combo of butter lettuce and other leaf lettuces, mostly light green to yellow to medium green
- Mediterranean—escarole, leaf lettuces, radicchio, and endive
- Field greens—leaf lettuce, curly endive, radicchio, and carrots

THE SECRET TO FAST INGREDIENTS

Speed up salad making easily with the help of a few fabulous machines, which are well worth the investment:

- Food processor—Emulsify a salad dressing; purée basil, oil, and garlic into a pesto; julienne carrots; chop onions; shred cabbage—the ways in which the processor cuts down salad-fixing time are endless.

5 IRRESISTIBLE FRUIT 'N' CHEESE COMBOS

Fruit and cheese complement each other perfectly. They work well with tossed greens in a decorative composed salad or even on a platter for a buffet or patio table. Here are some combinations that work well, complete with a description of each of the cheeses. For more on the blue cheeses that go with fruits, see page 139.

GREEK ISLE HOLIDAY: Feta surrounded with slices of fresh figs, ripe red Bartlett pears (with the skin left on), and spiced walnuts.

This traditional Greek cheese is made from sheep's and/or goat's milk. Since it's cured, then stored in its own salty whey, it's often referred to as pickled cheese (in its own whey, you can keep it stored up to 4 weeks in the refrigerator). Look for this white, crumbly cheese in small cakes that are perfect for a buffet fruit salad tray. Some feta even comes sprinkled with fresh herbs.

A TASTE OF ITALY: Mascarpone cheese with fresh raspberries and fresh blackberries with sugared walnuts sprinkled over all.

This delicate and buttery double-cream cheese comes from the agricultural farmlands of Italy's Lombardy region. Some mascarpones have the consistency of clotted cream, while others resemble room temperature butter. Some even come as extra-rich as triple cream cheeses, but all have that delicious whipped cream taste! (You might need to seek out a specialty gourmet cheese shop for this one.)

COPENHAGEN REPAST: Havarti with crisp slices of Granny Smith apples, red grapes, dried apricots, and spiced almonds.

Havarti hails from Denmark and is a semi-soft, incredibly buttery cheese with a characteristic golden to pale yellow interior. Look closely; it has many tiny irregular holes throughout. It's creamy and slightly tangy in flavor, with the mildest of taste when young, which sharpens as it ages.

FROM PARIS, WITH LOVE: A wedge of Brie, some dark bing cherries, slices of golden or honeydew melon, toasted walnuts—and voilà!

Since the 8th century, Brie has been enjoyed the world over. The classic one, known as Brie de Meaux, has a golden interior, a slightly stronger flavor, and is made from unpasteurized cow's milk. Those made from pasteurized milk in other regions of France (for the import market) and in the United States come in large wheels with a downy white rind, a buttery pale yellow interior that oozes at its peak of ripeness, and have a slightly tangy taste.

DOWN ON THE FARM: A chunk of farmhouse Cheddar, slices of Red Delicious apples, deep purple grapes, and ripe red strawberries.

The first Cheddars came from the village of Cheddar in the countryside of Somerset, England. Cheddar is now one of Britain's and America's favorite cheeses. Made from pasteurized cow's milk, this hard, dense cheese varies from ivory to deep pumpkin orange, from mild and almost sweet to deep sharp and full-bodied, which is associated with the mature farmhouse Cheddars.

- Cylinder food chopper—What's old is new again! This simple, inexpensive tool was one that our mothers and grandmothers loved for chopping all kinds of small items, and now it's back on the market. Perfect for chopping fresh herbs or garlic fast.
- Mandoline or vegetable slicer—Other great tools for slicing salad ingredients. The high-carbon steel blades adjust quickly and easily to give you the

exact slice you want—the thinnest of thin or the thickest of thick. Some of the less-expensive slicers come with fixed blades that are sharp and efficient.

- Mezzaluna—Its name means "half moon," and that's exactly what it looks like. This crescent-shaped cutter has one or two curved chopping blades with a vertical handle at each end. Just grab a handle in each hand and rock the blade back and forth over the food on a board.

LAYERING IN THE FLAVORS

Before you add the first ingredient to a salad, start by flavoring the salad bowl. Slice a large clove of garlic diagonally to give you the biggest cut surface possible and rub the inside of the bowl with the cut side of the garlic.

Now as you build the salad, season and spice as you go. For instance, toss leafy greens with a little cracked pepper, marinate tomatoes before tossing into the bowl, or pickle beets or cucumbers. Or quickly blanch the fresh vegetables in spiced water before tossing them into the bowl. Sprinkle in fresh herbs and drizzle on dressings. All these things keep layering in the flavor!

Now start browsing through the pages of *Satisfying Salads* and make a list of those you want to try. Here are a few favorites:

Americana Salad (page 20)

BLT Salad (page 37)

Classic California Cobb (page 54)

Catalina Seafood Salad (page 62)

French Potato Salad (page 92)

Light & Fruity Raspberry Mold (page 108)

Fruit Salad Lanai (page 123)

Cherry-Walnut Vinaigrette (page 126)

French Potato Salad, page 92

Cherry-Walnut Vinaigrette, page 126

Fresh Fruit Parfait Mold, page 110

Fruit & Cheese Salad, page 38

Mostly Greens

How exciting our salad bowls are these days! Even the old standby of iceberg lettuce is getting a makeover, dressed with a honey-dijon dressing or tossed into the salad bowl with greens like arugula, radicchio, or Bibb. Try the wilted spinach salad with the extra surprise of dried cranberries or our Quick Caesar Salad, which takes so little fixing, thanks to preshredded cheese and Italian greens from a bag. Blue cheese joins up with beets and romaine for one salad, while mozzarella tosses with baby lettuce and endive for another. And the best part . . . because many rely on prepackaged vegetables from the produce department, they are ready to serve in mere minutes!

ALMOND LETTUCE WEDGES WITH HONEY DIJON

Prep **15 MINUTES + CHILLING**

1   cup salad oil

¼   cup cider vinegar

DRESSING

1   tablespoon honey

2   tablespoons Dijon mustard

1   head iceberg lettuce

½   cup slivered or sliced almonds, toasted

Once you taste this dressing, you will want to make a double batch so it is at the ready. Just be sure to store the dressing in the refrigerator.

LET'S BEGIN Prepare the dressing: Put the oil, vinegar, honey, and mustard in a blender. Blend for 1 minute or until thoroughly combined. Cover and refrigerate.

FIX & CHILL Remove the core from the lettuce and discard. Rinse and drain the lettuce thoroughly. Cut into 6 wedges, wrap, and chill thoroughly, about 1 hour.

SPOON & SPRINKLE Arrange the lettuce wedges on 6 serving plates. Spoon the dressing over the wedges. Sprinkle with almonds and serve immediately.

Makes 6 servings

Per serving: 412 calories, 4g protein, 9g carbohydrates, 42g fat, 4g saturated fat, 0mg cholesterol, 128mg sodium

---

Cook to Cook

WHAT ARE SOME FAST AND EASY WAYS TO TOP A SALAD?

"I like to think that what's on top can be the most interesting part of a salad. Just a little something to add a bit of crunch, a hint of sweetness, a creamy counterpoint, or a wake-up call of intense flavor.

Croutons can add both flavor and crunch. I like to keep several varieties on hand and sometimes make my own by tossing cubes of pumpernickel, rye, brioche, or cornbread with oil and herbs and toasting them in a very low oven.

Other good sources of crunch are oyster crackers, the new miniature butter-flavored rounds, toasted nuts, and popcorn.

I often *sprinkle some berries, cherries, or cubes of fresh fruit* over a salad of mixed greens for a bit of color and a sweet surprise. Cubes of jicama are another favorite sweet topper.

Nothing beats *chunks of a creamy, melt-in-your mouth cheese* to top a crisp green salad with elegance. You don't have to bother toasting goat cheese on a bit of toast. Just cube some Brie or Camembert or crumble feta, ricotta salata, blue cheese, or goat cheese over the greens.

For a salad to remember, I like to add just *a little bit of something with big flavor*—a teaspoonful of salted capers, some rolled anchovies, a confetti of chopped pickled cherry peppers or jalapeños, some wasabi-coated peanuts or green peas, or a drizzle of salsa."

SuperQuick

CRANBERRY-SPINACH SALAD WITH DIJON BACON DRESSING

Prep **10 MINUTES**   *Microwave* **5 MINUTES**

Warm Honey Dijon–Bacon
  Dressing (see recipe)

1   package (6 ounces) baby
     spinach, stems trimmed,
     washed, and dried

½   cup dried cranberries

½   small red onion, thinly
     sliced

This sweet-savory dressing is also great on warm slices of roast chicken. If you prefer the bite taken out of the red onion, slice it, then let it soak in red wine vinegar to cover for 30 minutes.

LET'S BEGIN Prepare the Warm Honey Dijon–Bacon Dressing.

FIX IT FAST Divide the spinach evenly among 4 salad plates. Top each with 2 tablespoons sweetened dried cranberries and onion slices.

DRESS IT UP Drizzle each salad with 2 tablespoons dressing.

WARM HONEY DIJON–BACON DRESSING

Microwave 4 slices bacon (or turkey bacon) per manufacturer's instructions, until crisp. Cool, crumble, and put in a microwaveable bowl. Add ½ cup plain or orange-flavored honey, ½ cup lime juice, and 2 tablespoons Dijon mustard and whisk until blended. Microwave on high for 1 minute, or until warm. Makes 1 cup.

TIP: Store any extra dressing in a covered jar in the refrigerator up to 1 week. Warm before using.

Makes 4 servings
Per serving: 155 calories, 3g protein, 33g carbohydrates, 2g fat, 1g saturated fat, 3mg cholesterol, 206mg sodium

SuperQuick
AMERICANA SALAD

Prep **15 MINUTES**

Pineapple Dressing (see recipe)

1   **package (12 ounces) vegetable salad blend**

2   **cups broccoli florets**

1   **cup cauliflower florets**

1   **cup sliced celery**

1   **large red, green, or yellow bell pepper, cut into chunks**

The Pineapple Dressing really brightens the flavors of everyday vegetables. To prepare the dressing super-quick, put all of the ingredients in a covered container and shake it until the dressing emulsifies.

LET'S BEGIN Prepare the Pineapple Dressing.

DRESS IT UP Combine the remaining ingredients in a large bowl. Drizzle the dressing over the salad and toss to mix well.

PINEAPPLE DRESSING

Whisk together ⅓ cup pineapple orange juice, ¼ cup cider vinegar, 3 tablespoons grated Parmesan cheese, and 2 tablespoons vegetable oil in a small bowl until well blended.

Makes 8 servings

Per serving: 64 calories, 2g protein, 5g carbohydrates, 4g fat, 1g saturated fat, 2mg cholesterol, 67mg sodium

---

Salad Basics

THE BEST WAY TO CHOOSE & STORE GREENS

Want to know how to make the most delicious salad? Use the freshest greens possible and store them right. Here's a quick guide:

- Choose green-leafed lettuce that is crisp and firm without any brown spots or edges, which are a sign of age.
- For the most flavor, purchase greens with their roots still attached.
- Pick a head of iceberg lettuce

that feels heavy for its size. Iceberg with dark green leaves attached rather than a head of pale leaves is the preferred choice. It's better for you too.

- Store your salad fixings as soon as you get home.
- Remove any metal bands or rubber bands and, if needed, discard any outer leaves.
- Unwashed greens will last for about 3 days in the crisper drawer of your refrigerator.

- For longer storage, wash the greens using the directions in "Simple Advice for Washing & Drying the Greens" on page 22.
- Place the washed greens in a plastic bag with a few holes poked in it and place in the crisper drawer, or use a plastic container with a slatted tray at the bottom that is meant specifically for greens. Either way, the greens will keep crisp for 1 week.

SPINACH SALAD WITH CITRUS VINAIGRETTE

Prep **15 MINUTES**

Citrus Vinaigrette (see recipe)

1   package (16 ounces) fresh spinach, stems removed

1   small red onion, thinly sliced

1½   cups white mushrooms, sliced

¼   cup chopped bacon, cooked until crisp

Ground black pepper (optional)

Spinach, bacon, and mushroom salad is a classic combo. To save time, use packaged fully cooked bacon.

LET'S BEGIN Prepare the Citrus Vinaigrette.

TOSS & TASTE Place all of the remaining ingredients, except the pepper, in a large salad bowl. Pour the vinaigrette over the salad and lightly toss. Add pepper to taste, if you wish.

CITRUS VINAIGRETTE

Whisk together ½ cup orange juice, ¼ cup canola oil, 1 minced garlic clove, 2 tablespoons sugar, and 1 tablespoon white vinegar in a small bowl until blended well.

Makes 6 servings

Per serving: 140 calories, 5g protein, 8g carbohydrates, 11g fat, 1g saturated fat, 3mg cholesterol, 238mg sodium

---

Salad Basics

SIMPLE ADVICE FOR WASHING & DRYING GREENS

Preparing a crisp, flavorful, and beautiful salad is all about handling delicate greens properly. It's easy!

WASHING WITH TLC!

- Handle greens with tender loving care, as they bruise easily.
- Gently separate the leaves and place them in a large bowl or sink full of cold water. Swish them around with your hands to loosen any soil or grit.

- Lift the leaves from the water so the dirt remains in the bottom of the bowl or sink. Pour off the water and refill the bowl. Repeat the process until the water is perfectly clean and free of grit.

Tip: Some greens, such as leaf lettuces, may only require a single rinsing, while spinach or arugula may need to be washed several times.

SPIN-DRYING

It is important to dry greens well. A salad spinner is the best and easiest way to accomplish this.

- Do not overpack the spinner as this may bruise the leaves.
- Spin the greens until all of the excess moisture has been removed.
- If you don't have a salad spinner, shake the greens in a colander, then pat them dry between layers of paper towels.

ASIAN SPINACH SALAD

Prep **25 MINUTES**   *Cook* **8 MINUTES**

Sweet & Spicy Dressing (see recipe)

4   ounces dried rice noodles or rice sticks

4   cups torn fresh spinach

¾   cup dried tart cherries

⅓   cup chopped fresh mint leaves (or other fresh herbs)

2   medium carrots, shredded

1   medium cucumber, seeded and cut into matchstick strips

⅓   cup unsalted dry roasted peanuts

You will find dried rice noodles (also known as rice sticks) in the Oriental section of most supermarkets. These translucent noodles are appreciated for their light texture and delicate taste. Pay attention as they cook, since they take less time than pasta.

LET'S BEGIN Prepare the Sweet & Spicy Dressing and set aside.

COOK IT UP Cook the rice noodles or rice sticks in a large pot of boiling water for 2 to 6 minutes, until tender. Drain in a colander and immediately rinse with cold water. Drain and fluff with a fork. Cut up the noodles with kitchen shears. Rinse again with cold water. Drain and fluff with a fork.

DRESS IT UP Toss the drained noodles with the next 5 ingredients. Drizzle the dressing over the salad and toss until well mixed. Sprinkle with peanuts and serve immediately.

SWEET & SPICY DRESSING

Combine 2 tablespoons orange juice, 1 tablespoon rice vinegar, ½ finely chopped medium jalapeño pepper (2 teaspoons), 1 tablespoon peeled grated fresh ginger, 2 finely chopped garlic cloves, 1 teaspoon grated orange zest, and ¼ teaspoon ground black pepper in a small bowl. Whisk until well blended.

Makes 4 servings

Per serving: 286 calories, 7g protein, 52g carbohydrates, 7g fat, 1g saturated fat, 0mg cholesterol, 42mg sodium

SuperQuick

SPRINGTIME SPINACH SALAD

Prep **15 MINUTES**   *Microwave* **3 MINUTES**

8	ounces asparagus spears
¼	cup water
1	package (6 ounces) baby spinach or spinach and leaf salad blend
1	pint strawberries, hulled and sliced
1	cup thinly sliced red onion
⅔	cup crumbled feta or blue cheese
½	cup bottled raspberry vinaigrette or red wine vinaigrette

When buying asparagus, take a good look at them. They should be firm without any signs of withering and the bottoms of the spears should not be bone dry. When you get them home, especially if you are not using them the same day, cut off the ends of the spears and stand them in ½ inch of cold water in the refrigerator.

LET'S BEGIN Break off the woody ends of the asparagus (about 1 inch) and discard them. Cut the asparagus into 1-inch lengths and place in a microwaveable dish with the water. Microwave on High for 3 minutes. Immediately rinse the asparagus under cold water for 1 minute and drain well.

DRESS IT UP Place the asparagus and all of the remaining ingredients in a large bowl. Toss together and serve immediately.

Makes 6 servings

Per serving: 103 calories, 4g protein, 14g carbohydrates, 4g fat, 2g saturated fat, 15mg cholesterol, 491mg sodium

CALIFORNIA CLASSIC SALAD
WITH ROQUEFORT DRESSING

Prep **15 MINUTES**

Roquefort Dressing (see recipe)

1   package (16 ounces) classic iceberg salad

12   cherry tomatoes, quartered

1   stalk broccoli, cut into florets

1   cup drained canned garbanzo beans

1   can (2¼ ounces) sliced ripe black olives, drained

Breadsticks (optional)

Though Roquefort is a blue cheese produced in France, it becomes part of an American classic when paired with iceberg lettuce. And for good reason—it's absolutely delicious.

LET'S BEGIN Prepare the Roquefort Dressing.

DRESS IT UP Toss the remaining ingredients with the Roquefort Dressing in a large serving bowl. Serve immediately with breadsticks, if you wish.

ROQUEFORT DRESSING

Whisk together ⅓ cup olive or vegetable oil, 3 tablespoons white wine vinegar, 1 cup crumbled Roquefort or blue cheese (4 ounces), 1 teaspoon ground black pepper, ½ teaspoon salt, and 2 finely chopped garlic cloves in a small bowl until well blended.

> *Makes 8 servings*
>
> *Per serving: 202 calories, 6g protein, 13g carbohydrates, 15g fat, 4g saturated fat, 13mg cholesterol, 567mg sodium*

SuperQuick
QUICK CAESAR SALAD

Prep **10 MINUTES**

Caesar Dressing (see recipe)

6 cups (10 ounces) romaine lettuce leaves or Italian blend salad greens, torn

1 cup shredded Parmesan, mozzarella & Romano cheese blend (4 ounces)

½ cup garlic croutons

The only thing better than Caesar salad is a tasty Quick Caesar Salad. Make it a main-dish salad by topping with grilled chicken if you prefer.

LET'S BEGIN Prepare the Caesar Dressing in a large bowl.

DRESS IT UP Add the lettuce, ¾ cup cheese, and the croutons. Toss together lightly.

SPRINKLE & SERVE Arrange the salad on 4 serving plates. Sprinkle the remaining cheese over the salads.

CAESAR DRESSING

Combine ¼ cup olive oil, 2 tablespoons lemon juice, 1 minced garlic clove, ¾ teaspoon salt, and ¼ teaspoon ground black pepper in a bowl. Whisk in 2 tablespoons mayonnaise.

> **Makes 4 servings**
> Per serving: 353 calories, 12g protein, 12g carbohydrates, 29g fat, 7g saturated fat, 24mg cholesterol, 901mg sodium

---

Salad Basics

A HANDY WAY TO HANDLE SALAD SERVINGS

Trying to figure out how much salad to prepare for a given number of people can be tricky. After all, no one wants to be caught short of food. Being a generous host is part of the pleasure of serving food to family and friends. So to help you, here are some salad guidelines.

Coleslaw	About 1 cup per person
Fresh fruit salad	1 cup per person
Green salad	3 ounces or 1½ to 2 cups per person
Mixed green salad	2 cups per person
Macaroni salad	About 1 cup per person
Pasta salad	1 to 1½ cups per person
Potato salad	About 1 cup per person

BEET, WALNUT & BLUE CHEESE

Prep **10 MINUTES + CHILLING**

2   jars (16 ounces each) sliced beets, drained

Sweet-Hot Mustard Vinaigrette (see recipe)

6   large romaine leaves

6   tablespoons chopped walnuts, toasted

6   tablespoons crumbled blue cheese

Toasting walnuts may seem like an unneeded bit of work, but the few minutes it takes is really worth it. Toasting brings out the nuts' flavor and also makes them temptingly crisp.

LET'S BEGIN Place the beets in a shallow bowl and set aside. Prepare the Sweet-Hot Mustard Vinaigrette and pour over the beets, tossing gently. Cover and refrigerate for 1 hour.

ARRANGE & SERVE Line 6 salad plates with the romaine leaves and top each with a layer of the marinated beets. Sprinkle each salad with 1 tablespoon each walnuts and cheese.

SWEET-HOT MUSTARD VINAIGRETTE

Combine ¼ cup red wine vinegar, 6 tablespoons olive oil, 2 teaspoons sugar, 1 tablespoon sweet-hot mustard, ½ teaspoon salt, and ½ teaspoon ground black pepper in a small bowl. Whisk until well blended.

Makes 6 servings

Per serving: 252 calories, 5g protein, 13g carbohydrates, 21g fat, 4g saturated fat, 6mg cholesterol, 631mg sodium

SuperQuick
Avocado Garden Salad

Prep **20 minutes**

1	large ripe avocado, pitted, peeled, and cut into thin wedges
3	tablespoons lemon juice
6	cups torn mixed salad greens
3	medium tomatoes, cut into ¾-inch chunks
5	green onions, sliced
1	small cucumber, peeled to create strips and cut into ¾-inch chunks
1	teaspoon coarsely ground black pepper
½	teaspoon salt
⅓	teaspoon garlic powder

Save kitchen time by washing your salad greens ahead of time. Spin them dry, then store in a paper towel–lined resealable plastic bag. They will stay fresh and crisp.

LET'S BEGIN Brush the avocado wedges with 1 tablespoon lemon juice and set aside.

TOSS TOGETHER Thoroughly combine 2 tablespoons lemon juice with the remaining ingredients in a large serving bowl.

SERVE IT UP Arrange the avocado wedges on top of the salad like a starburst and serve immediately.

Makes 6 servings

Per serving: 84 calories, 3g protein, 9g carbohydrates, 5g fat, 1g saturated fat, 0mg cholesterol, 220mg sodium

SuperQuick
TOMATO, PROSCIUTTO & FRESH MOZZARELLA

Prep **20 MINUTES**

1   package (10 ounces)
     organic salad blend
     spring mix with herbs or
     baby lettuce salad
1   cup yellow and red pear or
     cherry tomatoes, halved
1½   ounces prosciutto, chopped
4   ounces fresh mozzarella
     cheese, drained and torn
     into bits
1   cup sliced red onion
1   cup croutons
¼   cup prepared balsamic
     vinaigrette dressing

If you don't use all the fresh mozzarella, store the leftover portion in a covered container of cool water in the refrigerator.

LET'S BEGIN Combine the first 6 ingredients in a large bowl.

DRESS IT UP Drizzle the dressing over the salad and toss until well mixed.

Makes 4 servings
Per serving: 240 calories, 12g protein, 15g carbohydrates, 15g fat, 4g saturated fat, 25mg cholesterol, 534mg sodium

SuperQuick
MIXED BABY GREENS WITH APPLE, BACON & STILTON

Prep **20 MINUTES**

Balsamic Vinaigrette (see
recipe)
1   package (4 ounces)
     organic mixed baby
     greens
½   cup walnuts, toasted
4   slices thick-cut bacon,
     chopped and cooked
     until crisp
2   ounces Stilton or other
     blue cheese, crumbled
1   small Gala or Fuji apple,
     thinly sliced

The Gala or the Fuji apple tastes great in this salad, but you can also use a different sweet apple, such as Golden Delicious.

LET'S BEGIN Prepare the Balsamic Vinaigrette. Place the greens in a salad bowl and drizzle with the vinaigrette. Toss to coat the leaves.

TOP & SERVE Divide the greens between 4 chilled salad plates, and sprinkle each serving with some walnuts, bacon, and cheese. Garnish with the apple slices and serve immediately.

BALSAMIC VINAIGRETTE

Combine 2 tablespoons balsamic vinegar, 1 teaspoon Dijon mustard, 1 teaspoon minced shallots, ¼ teaspoon salt, ⅛ teaspoon pepper, 3 tablespoons walnut oil, and 3 tablespoons extra-virgin olive oil in a jar with a tight-fitting lid. Shake until well blended.

Makes 4 servings
Per serving (using all the vinaigrette): 418 calories, 10g protein, 10g carbohydrates, 39g fat, 7g saturated fat, 21mg cholesterol, 630mg sodium

Tomato, Prosciutto & Fresh Mozzarella

GOLDEN GATE SALAD

Prep **15 MINUTES**

California Dressing (see recipe)

1   package (4 ounces) organic mixed baby greens

¼   cup fresh tarragon leaves

¼   cup sliced almonds, toasted

2   ounces mild goat cheese or feta cheese, crumbled

½   ripe avocado, pitted, peeled, and thinly sliced

8   dried apricots, preferably Turkish, cut into strips

A California-style salad if there ever was one! Here's the easiest way to toast almonds. Put them into a small skillet over medium heat and cook, tossing occasionally, until nice and golden. Remove them from the skillet, as they will continue to brown.

LET'S BEGIN Prepare the California Dressing. Place the greens in a large bowl. Add the fresh tarragon and toss.

DRESS IT UP Add about one-third of the dressing and toss until well mixed. Add the rest of the dressing if you wish.

ARRANGE & SERVE Spread out the greens mixture on a platter and scatter the almonds and cheese on top. Arrange the avocado around the edge. Sprinkle the apricots over the salad and serve immediately.

CALIFORNIA DRESSING

Combine 2 tablespoons tarragon vinegar, 2 teaspoons Dijon mustard, 1 teaspoon honey, ⅓ cup plus 1 tablespoon extra-virgin olive oil, ½ teaspoon dried tarragon (or 2 teaspoons fresh), ⅛ teaspoon salt, and freshly ground black pepper to taste in a jar with a tight-fitting lid. Shake vigorously until well blended.

Makes 4 servings

Per serving: 382 calories, 8g protein, 14g carbohydrates, 34g fat, 7g saturated fat, 15mg cholesterol, 200mg sodium

MARINATED GOAT CHEESE & TOMATO SALAD

Prep **20 MINUTES + MARINATING**   *Cook* **3 MINUTES**

½   cup olive oil

½   teaspoon crushed fennel
    seeds

½   teaspoon dried basil, or
    4 to 5 fresh basil leaves,
    torn

Coarsely ground black pepper

1   log (4 ounces) goat
    cheese

1   head Boston lettuce,
    separated into leaves

2   large tomatoes, cut into
    wedges

3   tablespoons lemon juice

1½ tablespoons honey

Pinch of salt

¼   cup chopped pecans or
    walnuts, toasted
    (optional)

It can be hard to cut neat slices from a log of fresh goat cheese. The easiest way is to take a length of (unflavored) dental floss, hold it taut in both hands, and cut down through the cheese. Fast and neat!

LET'S BEGIN Blend the oil, fennel, basil, and pepper in a pie plate. Slice the goat cheese into 8 rounds and lay them in the oil. Cover, refrigerate, and marinate for 2 to 3 hours.

FIX IT UP To serve, arrange the salad greens on 4 salad plates. Place several tomato wedges and 2 rounds of goat cheese on each plate, reserving the marinade.

DRESS IT UP Heat the lemon juice and honey in a small skillet over medium-low heat just long enough to liquefy the honey. Whisk this mixture and a pinch or two of salt into the reserved marinade. Drizzle over each salad. Garnish with chopped nuts, if you wish, and serve.

Makes 4 servings

Per serving: 415 calories, 10g protein, 12g carbohydrates, 37g fat, 11g saturated fat, 30mg cholesterol, 178mg sodium

Salad Basics

3 SIMPLE RULES FOR PAIRING SALADS & DRESSING

When it comes to trying to figure out what dressing to toss with which salad, there are a couple of simple tips to keep in mind:

- Thick and creamy dressings are best when matched with sturdy greens or hearty ingredients so they don't get weighed down by the dressing. For example, iceberg lettuce wedges are ideal with thick and chunky blue cheese dressing. The crisp lettuce can stand up to the heavy dressing, and the lettuce's crispness also complements the dressing's rich flavor.

- Simple and uncomplicated vinaigrettes work best with salads that are made up of many ingredients. For example, a beet and watercress salad that is topped with toasted walnuts is best tossed with a simple sherry vinaigrette, which will not detract from any of the salad ingredient flavors.

- Allow 1½ to 2 cups salad greens and about 3 tablespoons dressing per person. Use a little less dressing if it is a tangy vinaigrette and a little more if the dressing is creamy.

QUICK MANDARIN-CRANBERRY SALAD

Prep **15 MINUTES**

Rice Vinegar Dressing (see recipe)

1   package (12 ounces) mixed salad greens

1   cup dried cranberries

1   cup thinly sliced celery

1   green onion, thinly sliced

1   can (11 ounces) mandarin oranges, drained

½   cup chopped pecans

Serve this jewel-like salad over crisp greens to brighten up your holiday buffet.

LET'S BEGIN Prepare the Rice Vinegar Dressing.

DRESS IT UP Combine the salad ingredients in a large bowl. Drizzle with the dressing and toss gently to coat.

RICE VINEGAR DRESSING

Combine ¼ cup light or regular sesame oil, 2 tablespoons rice vinegar, 2 tablespoons finely chopped fresh parsley, 2 tablespoons sugar, ½ teaspoon Chinese five-spice powder, if you wish, ½ teaspoon salt, and a dash of hot-pepper sauce in a small bowl. Whisk until well blended.

Makes 4 servings

Per serving: 390 calories, 3g protein, 45g carbohydrates, 23g fat, 3g saturated fat, 0mg cholesterol, 336mg sodium

---

Food Facts

4 FAST WAYS TO A NUTRITION BOOST

That enticing bowl of greens you are about to serve is a good start for a nutritious meal. Most salad greens provide some Vitamin C and are very low in calories, but you can increase the "good for you" quotient in a big way with some of these nutrient-rich add-ins.

- The darker the greens, the more vitamins and minerals they are likely to include. Adding some dark green and red to your basic salad mix makes it prettier as well as more nutritious.

- Add some yellow and orange for Vitamin A. In addition to carrots, try slices of fresh or dried apricots, peaches, mangos, or papayas or cubes of roasted sweet potato or winter squash.

- Count on dairy products to add protein, calcium, and Vitamin D. Cheeses of all kinds can add flavor to the mix, and sour cream, yogurt, or buttermilk dressings tend to be lower in calories than oil-based dressings—as well as more nutritious.

- Traditional protein sources such as meat, poultry, seafood, legumes, and eggs bring with them B vitamins and a variety of minerals—be sure to add a little even if the salad isn't a main dish.

STRAWBERRY & STILTON ON MIXED GREENS

Prep **20 MINUTES + CHILLING**

- 2 cups hulled and sliced strawberries
- 2 tablespoons chopped fresh basil leaves
- 2 tablespoons raspberry vinegar
- ½ teaspoon sugar
- 1 teaspoon olive oil
- 1 teaspoon water
- 4 cups mixed salad greens
- ¼ cup crumbled Stilton or feta cheese

French bread (optional)

Stilton is often referred to as the "king of cheeses." It is produced in the town of Stilton, England. It's made from cow's milk and is allowed to ripen for 4 to 6 months, during which time it is skewered to encourage the growth of Penicillium roqueforti *mold, thus giving it its blue-green streaks.*

LET'S BEGIN Combine the first 4 ingredients in a medium bowl. Toss well to coat the berries. Cover and refrigerate for 1 hour.

SHAKE IT UP Strain the mixture through a sieve into a measuring cup and pour into a jar. Set the strawberries aside. Add the oil and water to the jar. Cover tightly and shake vigorously to make the dressing.

DRESS IT UP Arrange the greens on 4 individual salad plates. Top each with ¼ of the reserved berries, dressing, and cheese. Serve with French bread, if you wish.

Makes 4 servings
Per serving: 80 calories, 3g protein, 11g carbohydrates, 3g fat, 1g saturated fat, 5mg cholesterol, 212mg sodium

BLT Salad

SuperQuick
BLT Salad

Prep **20 MINUTES**

12	slices bacon, cooked until crisp
	Red Wine Vinaigrette (see recipe)
4	cups shredded romaine lettuce
16	dried tomato halves, drained if packed in oil, rehydrated if dried
8	ounces fresh white mushrooms, thinly sliced
¼	cup sliced green onions

Save time here by using fully cooked packaged bacon.

LET'S BEGIN Coarsely crumble the bacon and set aside. Prepare the Red Wine Vinaigrette.

DRESS IT UP In a large bowl, toss together the romaine, tomatoes, and mushrooms. Add the vinaigrette and toss with the salad mixture. Divide the salad evenly among 4 dinner plates and top each with bacon and green onion.

RED WINE VINAIGRETTE

Whisk together ¼ olive oil, 3 tablespoons red wine vinegar, and ⅛ teaspoon sugar in a small bowl until blended. Add salt and pepper to taste.

> **Makes 4 servings**
>
> *Per serving: 280 calories, 9g protein, 10g carbohydrates, 24g fat, 5g saturated fat, 15mg cholesterol, 320mg sodium*

GREEN & ORANGE WITH BLUE CHEESE

Prep **15 MINUTES + CHILLING**

½	cup sour cream
⅓	cup vegetable oil
	Zest and juice of ½ lemon
½	cup crumbled blue cheese
1	small garlic clove, minced
½	teaspoon dried dill weed
¼	teaspoon seasoned salt
8	cups assorted salad greens, torn into bite-size pieces
3	oranges, peeled and cut into bite-size pieces

Any blue cheese will be great in this dressing, but it's best to buy a chunk of cheese and crumble it yourself. Try Roquefort, Maytag Blue, or Stilton.

LET'S BEGIN Prepare the Blue Cheese Dressing: Put the sour cream in a small bowl and whisk in the next 6 ingredients. Cover and refrigerate for 30 minutes. Combine the salad greens and oranges in a large bowl. Cover and refrigerate.

DRESS IT UP Drizzle the dressing over the salad mixture and toss until well mixed. Serve immediately.

> **Makes 8 servings**
>
> *Per serving: 165 calories, 3g protein, 9g carbohydrates, 14g fat, 4g saturated fat, 11mg cholesterol, 163mg sodium*

PEAR & WALNUT SALAD WITH BLUE CHEESE
Prep **15 MINUTES**

Red Wine Vinaigrette (see recipe)

2   ripe medium pears, cored and sliced

2   tablespoons crumbled blue cheese

2   tablespoons chopped fresh parsley

2   tablespoons coarsely chopped walnuts

Pears and walnuts are a classic combination, but when you are at the market and the apples happen to look better than the pears, feel free to use them instead, or use a combination.

LET'S BEGIN Prepare the Red Wine Vinaigrette.

DRESS IT UP Add all the remaining ingredients and toss to coat. Divide the salad among 4 serving plates and serve immediately.

RED WINE VINAIGRETTE

Whisk together 2 tablespoons olive or vegetable oil, 1 tablespoon red wine vinegar, 1 teaspoon Dijon mustard, and ¼ teaspoon coarsely ground black pepper in a medium bowl.

> *Makes 4 servings*
>
> *Per serving: 150 calories, 2g protein, 14g carbohydrates, 11g fat, 2g saturated fat, 5mg cholesterol, 100mg sodium*

FRUIT & CHEESE SALAD
Prep **15 MINUTES**

6   cups mixed salad greens

1   red apple, cored and chopped

½   cup shredded sharp Cheddar cheese (2 ounces)

¼   cup golden or dark raisins

⅓   cup vinaigrette or salad dressing

Fruit and cheese are a marriage made in heaven. This salad makes a tasty first course before a chicken or pork dinner.

LET'S BEGIN Combine the salad greens, apple, cheese, and raisins in a large bowl.

DRESS IT UP Drizzle the vinaigrette over the salad and toss until well mixed.

> *Makes 6 servings*
>
> *Per serving: 141 calories, 4g protein, 12g carbohydrates, 10g fat, 3g saturated fat, 9mg cholesterol, 181mg sodium*

ANTIPASTO SALAD

Prep **15 MINUTES + CHILLING**

8	cups mixed salad greens
1	jar (10 ounces) marinated artichoke hearts, drained
1	package (8 ounces) mozzarella cheese, cut into strips
4	ounces salami or pepperoni, cut into strips
1	cup pitted ripe black olives
1	medium tomato, cut into wedges
⅓	cup drained roasted red bell peppers, cut into strips
1	cup prepared balsamic vinaigrette dressing, red wine vinaigrette, or olive oil vinaigrette dressing

Italian bread (optional)

Be Italian and enjoy this robust antipasto salad! Marinated artichoke hearts add lots of flavor here. Use the flavorful drained artichoke oil for brushing on grilled chicken or in your favorite vinaigrette.

LET'S BEGIN Toss all the ingredients except the dressing and blend in a large salad bowl. Cover and chill for about 1 hour.

DRESS IT UP Just before serving, drizzle the dressing over the salad and toss until well mixed. Serve with crusty Italian bread, if you wish.

Makes 4 servings

Per serving: 644 calories, 21g protein, 20g carbohydrates, 55g fat, 16g saturated fat, 67mg cholesterol, 2,175mg sodium

Perfect Pasta Salad Toss, page 65

The Main Event

Salads are more popular today than ever before. With a sliced steak, a pot of pasta, or some pieces of chicken, these salads step into the spotlight as the main event. Start with the Classic Chef's Salad, ready to eat in just 20 minutes, thanks to greens from a salad bar, shredded cheese from a bag, and ready-roasted meats from the deli. Find delicious new ways to toss up an easy tuna salad, make a taco salad more festive, and even a way to turn Waldorf salad into dinner. You might have several favorite salad recipes that would be perfect as an entrée, so look ahead to see how to quick-change them into a dinner-worthy entrée. With so many recipes at your fingertips, you'll find salads are truly satisfying.

BEEF, PASTA & ARTICHOKE SALAD

Prep **5 MINUTES + MARINATING**   *Broil* **16 MINUTES**

1   boneless beef top sirloin steak, cut 1 inch thick (about 1½ pounds)

4   cups tricolored corkscrew pasta, cooked, drained, and rinsed

1   can (14 ounces) quartered artichoke hearts, drained

1   large red bell pepper, cut into thin strips

1   cup small pitted ripe olives (optional)

2   tablespoons slivered fresh basil leaves

½   cup prepared balsamic vinaigrette

Round out this Italian-style main dish by beginning the meal with a sliced tomato and mozzarella salad, then ending it with bakery ricotta cheesecake and espresso. Delicioso!

LET'S BEGIN Preheat the broiler. Place the steak on a rack in a broiler pan so that the surface of the beef is 3 to 4 inches from the heat. Broil for 16 to 21 minutes for medium-rare to medium doneness, turning once. Remove from the broiler and let rest 10 minutes. Cut the steak lengthwise in half, then crosswise into thin slices.

TOSS & TURN Combine the steak, pasta, artichoke hearts, bell pepper, olives (if you wish), and basil in a large bowl. Add the vinaigrette and toss.

MARINATE IT Cover the salad and marinate in the refrigerator for at least 2 hours.

Makes 8 servings

Per serving: 305 calories, 30g protein, 21g carbohydrates, 11g fat, 3g saturated fat, 76mg cholesterol, 537mg sodium

SuperQuick
GRILLED LONDON BROIL SALAD

Prep **5 MINUTES**   *Broil* **15 MINUTES**

The robust flavor of balsamic dressing really complements the salad's bold flavors. If you like, top the salad with fat chunks of your favorite blue cheese.

1	cup balsamic vinaigrette dressing
½	cup honey Dijon mustard
¼	cup minced red onion
1	boneless beef top round or sirloin steak (about 2 pounds)
8	cups cut-up romaine lettuce leaves
1	tomato, cut into wedges
½	small cucumber, sliced (about 1 cup)

Olives (optional)

LET'S BEGIN Whisk together the first 3 ingredients. Set aside 1 cup in a covered jar in the refrigerator.

BROIL OR GRILL Preheat the broiler or heat the grill to medium. Broil or grill the steak, turning once and basting often with the remaining dressing, for 15 minutes for medium-rare, or until the steak is the way you like it. Slice the steak crosswise.

DRESS IT UP Place the lettuce, tomato, and cucumber on a large platter. Top with the sliced steak and drizzle with the reserved dressing. Garnish with olives, if you wish, and serve immediately.

Makes 8 servings

Per serving: 306 calories, 27g protein, 9g carbohydrates, 18g fat, 4g saturated fat, 71mg cholesterol, 300mg sodium

---

On the Menu

On a warm summer's day, what better way to keep the kitchen cool and guests happy than with a lovely London broil salad? Bring out a white tablecloth and set the table under the shade of an old oak tree.

Gazpacho

Fresh Garlic Bread

Grilled London Broil Salad

Mixed Heirloom Tomato Salad

Iced Tea

Lemon Sorbet with Mixed Berries

EASY TACO SALAD

Prep **15 MINUTES + CHILLING**   *Cook* **10 MINUTES**

1	pound 85% lean ground beef
1	package (1.25 ounces) taco seasoning
1	package (16 ounces) salad greens, or 1 cup torn iceberg lettuce and 1 cup shredded carrots
3	cups coarsely crushed tortilla chips
⅓	cup sliced ripe black olives
1	bottle (8 ounces) French salad dressing
2	cups nacho and taco-style shredded cheese (8 ounces)
2	tomatoes, cut into wedges
6	tablespoons sour cream

This is perfect food for your next Super Bowl party. It tastes fabulous and is oh so easy to prepare. Serve along with beer, your favorite dip and chips, and lots of warm cornbread.

LET'S BEGIN Prepare the ground beef, using the taco seasoning and following the directions on the package. Transfer to a large bowl and refrigerate for 10 minutes, or until cooled.

DRESS IT UP Add the lettuce, chips, and olives to the cooled beef in the bowl. Pour the salad dressing over the mixture and toss until well mixed.

TOP IT OFF Arrange the salad on serving plates. Top each salad with the cheese, tomato wedges, and a dollop of sour cream. Serve immediately.

Makes 6 servings

Per serving: 614 calories, 29g protein, 18g carbohydrates, 48g fat, 19g saturated fat, 112mg cholesterol, 1,424mg sodium

SuperQuick
CLASSIC CHEF'S SALAD

Prep **30 MINUTES**

6   cups salad greens
(10 ounces)

¼   pound thick-sliced
smoked cooked ham, cut
into ¼-inch strips

¼   pound thick-sliced oven
roasted turkey breast,
cut into ¼-inch strips

2   hard-cooked eggs,
quartered

1   large tomato, cut into
wedges

1½   cups shredded Cheddar
Jack cheese (6 ounces)

1   small cucumber, sliced
(optional)

½   cup sliced fresh white
mushrooms (optional)

½   cup Thousand Island or
French salad dressing

*No one is exactly sure who created the first chef's salad or where,
but it is known that it happened in America, and some believe
probably California. One thing all agree on is that it is a classic that
never wears out its welcome.*

LET'S BEGIN Line a serving platter with the greens.

FIX IT FAST Arrange the ham, turkey, eggs, and tomato
over the salad greens.

TOP & SERVE Top with the shredded cheese, cucumber,
and mushrooms, if you wish. Serve with your choice of
dressing.

Makes 4 servings

*Per serving: 406 calories, 25g protein, 14g carbohydrates,
30g fat, 11g saturated fat, 170mg cholesterol,
1,313mg sodium*

CITRUS PORK TENDERLOIN & SPINACH SALAD

Prep **15 MINUTES**　　*Bake* **30 MINUTES**

1　pork tenderloin
　　(1 pound)

Salt and pepper (optional)

½　cup orange juice

¼　cup sweet and tangy
　　honey mustard

12　cups baby spinach leaves
　　and/or mixed field
　　greens

1½　cups orange segments
　　(about 3 medium
　　oranges)

1⅓　cups french-fried onions

½　red bell pepper, cut into
　　strips

Pork tenderloin is a great cut of meat. It can be counted on to be juicy, flavorful, and tender. Be sure not to overcook the pork; 160°F means it is cooked to perfection.

LET'S BEGIN Preheat oven to 425°F. Place the tenderloin in a small roasting pan and season it with salt and pepper, if you wish.

INTO THE OVEN Bake the tenderloin for 30 minutes, or until the meat reaches an internal temperature of 160°F. Cool for 5 minutes, then cut into ¼-inch-thick slices. Combine the orange juice and mustard in a small bowl for the dressing and set aside.

DRESS IT UP Arrange the salad greens evenly on 6 serving plates. Top with pork, oranges, and onions, dividing evenly. Garnish each salad with red pepper. Drizzle the dressing over the salads and serve immediately.

Makes 6 servings

Per serving: 230 calories, 19g protein, 18g carbohydrates, 9g fat, 3g saturated fat, 49mg cholesterol, 280mg sodium

---

Salad Basics

TURNING SMALL SALADS INTO MAIN EVENTS

If you have all the ingredients for a basic salad, you are well on your way to making it a complete meal. Just increase the protein—that is, add more fish, meat, poultry, eggs, or cheese—and you've done it! Here are some ways to go:

- Basic green salad is the perfect foundation for large pieces of hot or cold grilled, sautéed, poached, or deep-fried meat, poultry, or fish. You don't have to go to a lot of trouble seasoning whatever you are adding.

The salad dressing will season and spice it up just fine.

- Basic garden salad pairs well with cold sliced meats or cheeses. Be sure to cut the pieces to match the size of the vegetables in the salad. Or, dice up all the ingredients and toss them all together for a hearty chopped salad.

- Basic Caesar salad can already contain anchovies, so shrimp, calamari, or other seafood is a perfect addition to make this favorite a meal. For a vegetarian alternative, just add some

chickpeas or beans and increase the traditional shower of shredded Parmesan cheese on top.

- Basic fruit salad takes well to salty and smoky additions such as slices of baked ham or smoked turkey. Gourmet cheese tucked into an arranged fruit salad is a classic combination.

- Basic slaw, whether all cabbage, broccoli, or mixed vegetables, is a delicious partner for shredded cooked meat or poultry or julienne strips of luncheon meats, cheese, and cooked sausages.

SuperQuick
DELUXE CHEF'S SALAD

Prep **25 MINUTES**

1	small head iceberg lettuce, torn
2	cups cut-up cooked chicken
½	pound cooked ham, cut into thin strips
1	cup cubed Cheddar or Swiss cheese (about 4 ounces)
2	tomatoes, cut into wedges
2	hard-cooked eggs, sliced
¾	cup prepared French dressing

A head of iceberg lettuce is preferred for this chef's salad because it has a softer head in comparison to the hard head of a cabbage. The softer heads contain more dark, leafy greens, which are tastier and better for you too.

LET'S BEGIN Place the lettuce in a salad bowl.

FIX IT FAST Arrange the next 5 ingredients over the lettuce.

DRESS IT UP Drizzle the dressing over the salad and toss.

Makes 6 servings

Per serving: 378 calories, 28g protein, 9g carbohydrates, 26g fat, 7g saturated fat, 143mg cholesterol, 973mg sodium

SuperQuick
BLT SALAD WITH BOW TIES

Prep **15 MINUTES**   *Cook* **15 MINUTES**

2	cups bowtie or corkscrew-shaped pasta (4 ounces)
1	package (9 ounces) romaine and radicchio salad blend or baby spinach salad
5	slices bacon, cooked until crisp and crumbled, or ⅓ cup packaged bacon bits
1	cup cherry, pear, or baby Roma tomatoes, halved
¾	cup diced Cheddar cheese (3 ounces)
⅓	cup ranch salad dressing

Perhaps the only thing better than a BLT sandwich is this salad. Or think of it as another way to enjoy this all-American combo. Use bowties, corkscrew pasta, or any of your favorite tube- or medium-sized pasta.

LET'S BEGIN Cook the pasta according to package directions. Drain, rinse in cold water, and drain again. Transfer to a large salad bowl.

DRESS IT UP Add the next 4 ingredients and toss to mix. Pour the dressing over the salad and toss again until evenly coated.

Makes 3 servings

Per serving: 519 calories, 21g protein, 47g carbohydrates, 29g fat, 10g saturated fat, 43mg cholesterol, 791mg sodium

Tangy Tuna Macaroni Salad

Prep **15 MINUTES**   *Cook* **13 MINUTES + CHILLING**

- **2   cups elbow macaroni**
- **1   can (6 ounces) tuna, drained**
- **2   celery ribs, sliced (1 cup)**
- **3/4   cup mayonnaise**
- **1/4   cup chopped green bell pepper**
- **1/4   cup sliced scallions**
- **2   tablespoons chopped pimiento**
- **Salt and ground black pepper**

The tangy taste of this pasta salad is thanks to the salad dressing (also known as Miracle Whip). Make it with tuna as in this recipe one day and vary it other times by substituting a cup of cubed ham or diced cooked chicken or turkey.

LET'S BEGIN Cook the pasta according to package directions. Drain, rinse under cold running water and drain again.

TOSS & CHILL Combine the pasta and the next 6 ingredients in a large bowl. Season to taste with salt and pepper. Cover and refrigerate for several hours or overnight.

Makes 8 servings

Per serving: 170 calories, 8g protein, 23g carbohydrate, 5g total fat, 1g saturated fat, 15mg cholesterol, 310mg sodium

CARAMELIZED APPLE SALAD WITH GRILLED CHICKEN

Prep **20 MINUTES**   *Cook* **25 MINUTES**   *Grill* **10 MINUTES**

¼   cup cholesterol-free butter-type spread

1   large Granny Smith apple or other tart apple, peeled, cored, and thinly sliced

1   large onion, sliced

2   cooked boneless, skinless chicken breast halves (about 8 ounces)

4   cups mixed salad greens or mesclun

¼   cup prepared balsamic vinaigrette dressing

½   cup toasted chopped walnuts or pecans (optional)

Cooking the apple and onion in butter until golden brown is known as caramelizing. This slow cooking allows the foods' natural sugars to develop, making their flavor rich and satisfying. For the most flavor, grill or broil the chicken.

LET'S BEGIN In a 12-inch skillet, melt the butter spread over medium-high heat. Cook the apple and onion, stirring occasionally, for 4 minutes or until tender. Reduce the heat to medium and cook uncovered, stirring occasionally, for 20 minutes, or until golden brown.

FIRE UP THE GRILL Meanwhile, heat the grill to medium or preheat the broiler. Grill or broil the chicken, turning once, about 10 minutes, or until no longer pink in the center. Slice the chicken ½-inch thick and keep warm.

DRESS IT UP Line 2 plates with the greens. Spoon the warm apple mixture over the greens and top with the chicken. Drizzle with the dressing and garnish with walnuts, if you wish. Serve immediately.

Makes 2 servings

Per serving: 516 calories, 29g protein, 27g carbohydrates, 33g fat, 5g saturated fat, 66mg cholesterol, 753mg sodium

California Chicken Salad

Prep **10 MINUTES**

- 3 cups cubed cooked chicken breast
- 2 cups cherry tomatoes, halved
- 3 green onions, chopped
- ⅓ cup prepared horseradish
- ⅓ cup bacon sour cream dip
- ½ teaspoon salt
- ½ teaspoon ground black pepper
- 2 avocados, peeled, pitted, and sliced

Chances are the avocados in your market are not ripe. So plan ahead and shop for them a couple of days before you plan to make this salad. An avocado is ripe when it yields to gentle pressure.

LET'S BEGIN Toss together the first 5 ingredients in a medium bowl. Season with the salt and pepper.

ARRANGE & SERVE Decoratively place the avocado slices on 4 salad plates. Top with the chicken salad and serve.

Makes 4 servings

Per serving: 410 calories, 37g protein, 15g carbohydrates, 23g fat, 6g saturated fat, 100mg cholesterol, 660mg sodium

FARMERS' MARKET CHICKEN SALAD

Prep **35 MINUTES**   *Bake* **12 MINUTES**

Honey-Dijon Dressing (see recipe)

1½   cups toasted wheat germ

1   teaspoon garlic powder

1   teaspoon salt

½   teaspoon ground black pepper

3   large egg whites

2   tablespoons water

1   pound boneless, skinless chicken breasts, cut into 1-inch-wide strips

6   cups mixed salad greens, torn into bite-size pieces

2   cups red or yellow cherry tomatoes, halved

1½   cups assorted vegetables, such as thin green beans or snow peas, cucumbers or sliced bell peppers

The crunch of the toasted wheat germ coating on the chicken makes it delicious, but if you are short on time, buy a deli-roasted chicken and tear the meat into chunks.

LET'S BEGIN Prepare the Honey-Dijon Dressing. Cover and refrigerate until ready to use. Heat the oven to 400°F. Coat a large baking sheet with cooking spray. Combine the next 4 ingredients in a shallow dish. Beat the egg whites with the water in a shallow dish until frothy.

DIP AND BAKE Dip the chicken into the egg, then into the wheat germ mixture. Dip and coat each piece again to coat thoroughly. Place on the prepared baking sheet and coat lightly with cooking spray. Bake for 12 to 15 minutes, or until the chicken is no longer pink in the center.

DRESS IT UP Arrange the remaining ingredients on a serving platter, top with the warm chicken, and drizzle with the dressing. Serve immediately.

HONEY-DIJON DRESSING

Combine ¼ cup honey, ¼ cup balsamic vinegar, 3 tablespoons Dijon mustard, 1 tablespoon chopped fresh thyme, ¼ teaspoon ground black pepper, and 1 tablespoon vegetable oil in a small bowl, mixing well.

Makes 4 servings

Per serving: 450 calories, 42g protein, 52g carbohydrates, 11g fat, 2g saturated fat, 65mg cholesterol, 980mg sodium

WALDORF CHICKEN SALAD

Prep **20 MINUTES + MARINATING**

Honey Dressing (see recipe)

12 dried apricots

2 cups cooked chicken or turkey, cut into cubes

2 apples, cored and diced

1 cup diced celery

⅓ cup toasted sliced almonds

¼ cup finely chopped green onion

The very first Waldorf Salad was created in New York City in 1893 at the Waldorf-Astoria Hotel. The original recipe contained red apples, celery, and mayonnaise—that's all! Later on, walnuts were added. And now this one gets even fancier with a honey 'n' poppy seed dressing.

LET'S BEGIN Prepare the Honey Dressing in a large salad bowl.

SOAK IT UP Add the apricots and let stand for 30 minutes. Remove the apricots from the dressing and set aside.

TOSS & CHILL Add the remaining ingredients to the dressing and toss lightly. Garnish with the reserved apricots. Serve or cover and refrigerate.

HONEY DRESSING

Whisk together ¼ cup honey, 2 tablespoons Dijon mustard, 1 tablespoon poppy seeds, ⅓ cup lemon juice, ½ teaspoon grated lemon zest, and ¼ cup salad oil in a large bowl until well blended.

Makes 6 servings

Per serving: 325 calories, 18g protein, 31g carbohydrates, 16g fat, 2g saturated fat, 40mg cholesterol, 184mg sodium

CLASSIC CALIFORNIA COBB

Prep **30 MINUTES**

1 ripe avocado, peeled, seeded, and chopped

1 tablespoon lemon juice

8 slices bacon, cooked until crisp and crumbled

1 package (10 ounces) mixed salad greens

2 boneless, skinless chicken breast halves, grilled and chopped

4 plum tomatoes, quartered

½ cup crumbled blue cheese (about 2 ounces)

2 hard-cooked eggs, chopped

4 green onions, sliced

½ cup roasted garlic vinaigrette dressing

Ever since the first Cobb salad was tossed together in 1937, the name has become synonymous with a chicken salad in which every-thing is chopped—with a little bit of this and a little bit of that. Though the ingredients vary in some versions today, this is the authentic way, with cooked breast of chicken, chopped avocado, hard-cooked eggs, and tomatoes. As salad, it's all tossed and dressed with a classic vinaigrette.

LET'S BEGIN Toss the avocado with the lemon juice in a large salad bowl.

TOSS Add all remaining ingredients except the dressing and mix lightly.

DRESS IT UP Divide the salad among 4 plates and drizzle with the dressing.

Makes 4 servings

Per serving: 420 calories, 5g protein, 15g carbohydrates, 28g fat, 9g saturated fat, 180mg cholesterol, 940mg sodium

---

Food Facts

THE BEGINNING OF THE CALIFORNIA COBB SENSATION

The year was 1937. The place, a famous Hollywood restaurant called The Brown Derby. Owner Bob Cobb and his friend Sid Grauman (of Grauman's Chinese Theatre) were hungry, but it was midnight and the chef had gone home. So Bob opened the big refrigerator and began pulling out "a little of this and a little of that."

What he found was: some cold breast of chicken, a hard-boiled egg, an avocado, some romaine, some watercress, a few tomatoes, some cheese, some chives, a head of lettuce, and some of that old-fashioned French dressing. Then he started chopping and chopping, adding some crisp bacon along the way. Bob Cobb's spur-of-the-

moment creation was rated "so good" by Grauman that he returned the next day and asked for it again. That chopped salad was well on its way to becoming an overnight sensation! Soon the Cobb Salad became a regular item on The Brown Derby menu. And that's how one more American classic was born.

CHICKEN & WILD RICE SALAD

Prep **30 MINUTES**   *Cook* **25 MINUTES + CHILLING**

Asian Dressing (see recipe)

1   package (6 ounces) long grain and wild rice mix

2   cups cubed cooked chicken

1   cup snow pea pods, cut crosswise in half and cooked

½   cup dried tart cherries

What a beautiful and delicious salad this is! It is best prepared ahead so all of the good flavors have a chance to blend, but be sure to remove it from the refrigerator about 30 minutes before serving so it isn't served too chilled.

LET'S BEGIN Prepare the Asian Dressing and set aside. Make the rice following package directions and let it cool for 15 minutes.

MIX & CHILL Combine the cooked chicken, snow peas, and dried cherries. Pour the dressing over the chicken mixture, mixing well. Stir the rice into the chicken mixture. Cover and chill for at least 1 hour before serving.

ASIAN DRESSING

Combine ¼ cup olive oil, 3 tablespoons soy sauce, 3 tablespoons lemon juice, 1½ teaspoons ground ginger, and ⅛ teaspoon ground black pepper in a small bowl, mixing well.

Makes 4 servings
Per serving: 470 calories,
27g protein, 53g carbohydrates,
17g fat, 3g saturated fat,
60mg cholesterol, 1,505mg sodium

SuperQuick
SHRIMP SALAD WITH DRIED CHERRIES
Prep **15 MINUTES**

Dijon Dressing (see recipe)

4 cups mixed salad greens

1 pound medium shrimp, peeled, deveined, and cooked

2 small ripe avocados, peeled, pitted, and sliced

¾ cup dried tart cherries

¼ cup sliced green onions

Save time by purchasing already peeled and cooked shrimp. For just a little more money, you will save lots of kitchen time. The dressing uses 2 tablespoons lemon juice, which is about 1 large lemon. To get the most juice, roll the lemon back and forth on the counter, pressing lightly with the palm of your hand.

LET'S BEGIN Prepare the Dijon Dressing. Divide the salad greens evenly among 4 plates.

FIX IT FAST Gently stir the shrimp, avocados, cherries, and green onions in a large bowl. Divide the shrimp mixture evenly over the salad greens.

DRESS IT UP Drizzle each salad with dressing and serve immediately.

DIJON DRESSING

Combine ⅓ cup olive oil, 2 tablespoons lemon juice, 1 teaspoon coarse-grained Dijon mustard, 1 teaspoon dried (or 1 tablespoon fresh) basil, and ¼ teaspoon salt in a small bowl. Mix with a wire whisk until well combined.

Makes 4 servings
Per serving: 538 calories, 27g protein, 39g carbohydrates, 33g fat, 5g saturated fat, 172mg cholesterol, 378mg sodium

TUNA SALAD ELEGANTE
Prep **30 MINUTES**

1	round bread loaf (about 1½ pounds)

Mayonnaise Dressing (see recipe)

1	can (12 ounces) tuna, packed in water, drained and flaked
6	spears asparagus, trimmed, cut into 2-inch pieces, and cooked
2	hard-cooked eggs, chopped
½	cup sliced pitted ripe black olives
½	cup sliced pimiento-stuffed green olives
⅓	cup chopped green onions
6	to 8 large lettuce leaves

Crackers or party bread (optional)

Lining a hollowed-out bread with lettuce, then spooning in salad is a fun and pretty way to enjoy this tuna salad. Use the soft center of the bread to make flavorful fresh bread crumbs. Let the bread dry out a little, then pulse it in a food processor until crumbs form.

LET'S BEGIN With a sharp knife, cut a 1-inch-thick slice from the top of the bread loaf. Save the top to use later for the lid. Hollow out the loaf to make a 1-inch shell. If preparing it ahead, wrap the shell and bread top in plastic wrap. Save the bread removed from the loaf for another use.

TOSS IT UP Prepare the Mayonnaise Dressing. Toss the next 6 ingredients with the dressing in a large bowl.

FILL & SERVE Line the bread shell with the lettuce leaves. Spoon the tuna mixture into the shell. Add the bread top. Serve with flat crackers or party bread, if you wish.

MAYONNAISE DRESSING

Stir together ⅓ cup reduced-calorie mayonnaise (or salad dressing), ¼ cup plain low-fat yogurt, 2 tablespoons red wine vinegar, 1 teaspoon crushed dried tarragon, and 1 teaspoon crushed dried basil in a small bowl. If preparing ahead, cover and chill.

Makes 5 servings

Per serving: 565 calories, 34g protein, 75g carbohydrates, 14g fat, 3g saturated fat, 110mg cholesterol, 1,569mg sodium

TASTY TUNA SALAD

Prep **15 MINUTES + CHILLING**

No need to worry about fresh lemons for this easy recipe; lemon and pepper seasoning salt adds all the lemon flavor needed here. The salad tastes best if refrigerated for 30 minutes, but you can prepare it up to 3 hours ahead.

1	can (6⅛ ounces) chunk-style tuna, packed in water, drained and flaked
2	tablespoons mayonnaise
2	tablespoons chopped celery
1	teaspoon dried minced onions
¾	teaspoon lemon and pepper seasoning salt
6	large lettuce leaves
2	tomatoes, cut into wedges

Lemon slices (optional)

LET'S BEGIN Stir the tuna, mayonnaise, celery, minced onion, and seasoning salt in a small bowl until well mixed. Cover and refrigerate for at least 30 minutes.

SERVE IT FAST Arrange the lettuce on 2 plates. Spoon half the tuna mixture in the center of each. Arrange tomato wedges around the tuna and garnish with lemon slices, if you wish.

Makes 2 servings

Per serving: 229 calories, 21g protein, 4g carbohydrates, 14g fat, 1g saturated fat, 41mg cholesterol, 606mg sodium

---

Cook to Cook

HOW DO YOU MAKE GREAT TUNA SALAD?

"I love preparing tuna salad for several reasons. It is a favorite of most adults and kids, it is easy on the wallet, and there are many tasty and easy ways to vary a basic tuna salad to guarantee your family will never get bored. Here are a few of my favorite tuna twists:

Begin with a can of drained and flaked tuna. Stir in a nice rib of *finely chopped celery; a couple of tablespoons chopped red or white onion, scallion, or chives;* the juice of half a large lemon; and a generous dollop of mayonnaise. To vary this basic recipe, toss in a tablespoon of *chopped drained capers and ¼ cup black or green olives,* chopped well.

For my second variation, I like to add 1 coarsely grated *hard-cooked egg, 1 coarsely grated carrot,* and about ¼ cup coarsely chopped parsley.

At other times, I like to toss in ½ *red bell pepper diced, 1 cup 1-inch lengths of cooked green beans, and ½ cup halved cherry tomatoes,* along with about 1 tablespoon Dijon mustard."

SEAFOOD SALAD WITH WHITE GRAPEFRUIT VINAIGRETTE

Prep **15 MINUTES**   *Broil* **4 MINUTES + CHILLING**

Grapefruit Vinaigrette (see recipe)

16   large shrimp (about ¾ pound), shelled and deveined, tails left on

12   sea scallops (about ¾ pound)

¼   cup sliced green onions

Leaving the tails on the shrimp makes for a lovely presentation, but if you prefer not to fuss with the tails when enjoying the salad, feel free to remove them.

LET'S BEGIN Prepare the Grapefruit Vinaigrette. Measure out ¼ cup for broiling the seafood and refrigerate the remaining vinaigrette for several hours to blend the flavors.

BROIL IT FAST Line a rimmed baking sheet with aluminum foil. Rinse the shrimp and scallops in cold water and drain well. Place them on the prepared baking sheet. Brush seafood with the reserved ¼ cup vinaigrette. Broil 3 to 4 inches from heat for about 4 to 6 minutes, turning once. The scallops should be opaque and the shrimp should look pink and cooked through.

CHILL & SERVE Place the cooked seafood in a medium bowl, cover, and refrigerate until chilled. To serve, divide the seafood among 4 individual plates. Pour the vinaigrette over the seafood and sprinkle with the green onions.

GRAPEFRUIT VINAIGRETTE

Mix ½ cup white grapefruit juice, 2 tablespoons pineapple juice, 1 tablespoon vegetable oil, 1 teaspoon sesame seeds, ⅛ teaspoon garlic powder, ½ teaspoon grated lemon zest, a pinch of ground white pepper, and a pinch of ground ginger in a small covered container.

Makes 4 servings

Per serving: 220 calories, 32g protein, 8g carbohydrates, 6g fat, 1g saturated fat, 157mg cholesterol, 264mg sodium

CATALINA SEAFOOD SALAD

Prep **35 MINUTES**

Catalina Dressing (see recipe)

¾   cup small shrimp, peeled, deveined, cooked, and chilled

¾   cup sea scallops, cooked, cut in half, and chilled

½   cup crabmeat, picked over and chilled

¾   cup thinly sliced plums

½   cup thinly sliced pineapple

½   cup thinly sliced honeydew or cantaloupe

½   cup thinly sliced red or green bell pepper

1   tablespoon finely chopped fresh parsley

Juice of 1 large lemon

2   cups mixed salad greens

The combination of shrimp, scallops, and crabmeat in this salad is great, but you can also use cooked mussels or lobster meat if you like.

MIX IT UP Prepare the Catalina Dressing. Combine the next 8 ingredients in a large bowl. Drizzle the lemon juice over all and toss to coat. Add the dressing and toss gently to combine.

TOP & SERVE Arrange the greens on a serving platter. Top with the seafood mixture and serve immediately.

CATALINA DRESSING

Combine 1 cup prepared Catalina-style salad dressing and 1 tablespoon tropical fruit juice concentrate in a glass measuring cup.

Makes 6 servings

Per serving: 275 calories, 10g protein, 16g carbohydrates, 20g fat, 2g saturated fat, 47mg cholesterol, 515mg sodium

SALADE À LA NIÇOISE
Prep **15 MINUTES**

Boston or romaine lettuce leaves

1   **package (9 ounces) frozen Italian green beans, cooked and drained**

4   **medium potatoes, cooked, peeled, and thinly sliced**

4   **medium tomatoes, sliced**

8   **hard-cooked eggs, sliced**

¼   **cup pitted ripe black olives, sliced**

¼   **cup reduced-fat or nonfat Italian dressing**

This recipe proves that a fantastic Niçoise salad can be prepared without tuna. Lots of tasty hard-cooked eggs provide all the protein you need.

LET'S BEGIN Arrange the lettuce attractively on 4 salad plates and spoon about ½ cup beans in the center of each.

LAYER IT ON Arrange the potato, tomato, and egg slices around the beans.

DRESS IT UP Sprinkle the olive slices over each salad and drizzle with the dressing.

> *Makes 4 servings*
>
> *Per serving: 330 calories, 17g protein, 38g carbohydrates, 12g fat, 3g saturated fat, 424mg cholesterol, 438mg sodium*

Food Facts

A FRENCH CLASSIC: SALADE À LA NIÇOISE

Foods that are prepared *à la Niçoise* (knee-SWAHZ) reflect how foods are typically prepared in and near the French Riviera city of Nice.

These dishes usually contain garlic, tomatoes, anchovies, black olives, capers, and lemon juice. Salad Niçoise is the most famous of these dishes. It classically consists of potatoes, canned tuna, olives, green beans, hard-cooked eggs, and vinaigrette dressing. Its "proper" assembly is a matter of opinion.

Some say this salad should be served on a bed of lettuce, while others say that tomatoes should be the base. Most often the elements of the salad are artfully arranged, but sometimes the ingredients are casually tossed together.

SuperQuick
CALIFORNIA CHOPPED SALAD
Prep **30 MINUTES**

8	cups torn romaine lettuce
1½	cups shredded sharp Cheddar cheese (6 ounces)
1	cup diced tomatoes
1	cup diced cooked chicken or turkey
½	cup crumbled cooked bacon
2	hard-cooked eggs, chopped (optional)
½	cup garlic croutons
1	ripe avocado, peeled, seeded, and diced
½	cup light Caesar salad dressing

Freshly ground black pepper (optional)

Save time by using deli-sliced turkey or a deli-roasted chicken. Give this salad lots of flavor by using a good-quality smoked bacon.

LET'S BEGIN Combine the lettuce, 1 cup cheese, the tomatoes, chicken, and bacon, plus eggs if you wish, in a large bowl. Serve immediately or cover and refrigerate for up to 4 hours.

DRESS IT UP Just before serving, add the croutons and avocado to the lettuce mixture. Add the dressing and toss lightly to coat all ingredients. Top with the remaining ½ cup cheese and serve with freshly ground pepper to taste, if you wish.

> *Makes 4 servings*
>
> *Per serving: 252 calories, 5g protein, 23g carbohydrates, 13g fat, 2g saturated fat, 1mg cholesterol, 485mg sodium*

EGG SALAD
Prep **20 MINUTES + CHILLING**

½	cup mayonnaise
¼	cup mustard
½	teaspoon paprika
12	hard-cooked eggs, coarsely chopped
1	cup sliced green onions

A freshly prepared bowl of egg salad is as perfect as food gets. It's great served along with crispy potato chips and lots of sliced pickles.

LET'S BEGIN Blend the mayonnaise, mustard, and paprika in a medium bowl.

MIX IT UP Gently stir in the eggs and green onions until they are blended. Refrigerate for at least 1 hour to blend the flavors.

> *Makes 6 servings*
>
> *Per serving: 235 calories, 13g protein, 8g carbohydrates, 17g fat, 4g saturated fat, 428mg cholesterol, 394mg sodium*

PERFECT PASTA SALAD TOSS

Prep **20 MINUTES**   *Cook* **10 MINUTES + CHILLING**

8   ounces penne pasta

4   ounces sliced salami, cut
     into strips

1   jar (7 ounces) roasted
     red peppers, drained and
     cut into thin strips

1   jar (6½ ounces)
     marinated, quartered
     artichoke hearts, drained

⅓   cup halved, pitted
     kalamata olives

¼   cup sliced fresh basil
     leaves

½   cup Italian or Caesar
     salad dressing

1   cup shredded Parmesan,
     mozzarella, and Romano
     cheese blend (4 ounces)

Romaine lettuce leaves
(optional)

To easily and quickly slice fresh basil leaves, stack the washed and dried basil leaves, then roll them up cigar-style. With a sharp knife, cut down through the roll, making the slices any thickness you desire.

LET'S BEGIN Cook the pasta following the package directions. Drain in a colander, rinse with cold water, and drain again.

DRESS IT UP Combine the salami, roasted peppers, artichoke hearts, olives, and basil in a large bowl. Add the pasta along with the salad dressing and cheese. Toss until well mixed.

CHILL & SERVE Cover the salad and refrigerate it for at least 30 minutes or up to 6 hours before serving. Serve the salad on lettuce leaves, if you wish.

Makes 4 servings

Per serving: 620 calories, 24g protein, 52g carbohydrates, 37g fat, 11g saturated fat, 50mg cholesterol, 1,489mg sodium

Time Savers

5 WAYS TO A FASTER PASTA SALAD

Everyone likes pasta salads. The only problem is getting that pasta cooked, cooled, and tossed in time for dinner. Here are some quick-cooking tips that help the fixing go faster.

- Fast cook: Heat the cooking water in several pots to bring it to a boil quickly; then combine them. Select smaller pasta shapes that will cook in less time.

- Jiffy chill: Cool cooked pasta in a bowl of ice cubes, in a colander under cool running water, or spread out on a tray, covered, in the freezer—or toss it with frozen corn or peas as it is draining.

- Batch it: Cook twice as much pasta as needed one evening for dinner; toss one batch with a little dressing and chill for the next night's salad.

- Cook and freeze: Pasta freezes very well. Cook several boxes at once and freeze it in batches. Toss the frozen pasta with warm dressing and set it aside; fold in the other ingredients just before serving.

- Serve warm: There's nothing wrong with serving a freshly made pasta salad either warm or at room temperature.

Mexican Chopped Salad, page 78

Spice It Up!

Neighbors around the globe, both near and far, love to serve spicy and spectacular salads, so here are some of the very best. Grill a beef steak flavored with fresh lemon as they do in Greece, then toss with greens and other veggies and top with feta and olives for a typical Mediterranean feast. Or chop up meat, veggies, and cheese as they do in Sicily, dress a vegetable-layered salad with salsa as is done in Mexico, or stir-fry shrimp for a cabbage salad as in Thailand. When it's tomato season, buy the ripest ones you can find, and toss them Italian-style with some balsamic vinaigrette topped with Parmesan shavings. They're all simple, easy, and fast—the real Quick Cook way.

Mexican Cobb Salad

Prep **20 MINUTES + CHILLING**

6   cups torn Romaine lettuce leaves

1½   cups shredded Mexican-style four-cheese blend (6 ounces)

1¾   cups diced cooked chicken or cooked baby shrimp

1   small tomato, diced (1 cup)

⅓   cup thinly sliced scallions

6   slices crumbled cooked bacon

½   cup sliced ripe black olives or diced avocado (optional)

⅓   cup salsa

¼   cup light mayonnaise

Here's a south-of-the-border version of the original Cobb Salad, which was created one night in 1937 by Bob Cobb of the Brown Derby Restaurant in Hollywood. The original was all tossed together with a little bit of this and a little bit of that. But this one's all dressed up, beautifully arranged, and ready for a party. Just toss it up right before serving, if you like.

LET'S BEGIN Arrange the lettuce on a large serving platter.

LET IT CHILL Arrange the cheese, chicken, tomato, scallions, bacon, and olives, if desired, in a striped pattern over the lettuce. Combine the salsa and mayonnaise in a small bowl. Cover the salad and the dressing and refrigerate for 15 minutes, or until chilled.

TOP & SERVE Right before serving, add the dressing to the salad and toss to mix well.

Makes 6 servings

Per serving: 545 calories, 47g protein, 14g carbohydrates, 34g fat, 16g saturated fat, 152mg cholesterol, 1,277mg sodium

THAI BEEF SALAD

Prep **20 MINUTES + MARINATING**   *Grill* **15 MINUTES**

If you feel like jazzing up this tasty salad even further, top it with some chopped ripe tomato and chopped fresh cilantro—very Thai!

Thai Dressing (see recipe)

1   **flank steak (about 1½ pounds)**

6   **cups washed and torn mixed salad greens**

1   **cup sliced peeled cucumber**

⅓   **cup chopped unsalted peanuts**

LET'S BEGIN Prepare the Thai Dressing. Set aside 1 cup for dressing the salad. Place the steak in a large resealable food storage bag. Pour the remaining dressing over the steak. Seal the bag and refrigerate for 30 minutes to marinate.

FIRE UP THE GRILL Heat the grill to medium or preheat the broiler. Grill or broil the steak about 15 minutes, turning once, for medium-rare. Let stand 5 minutes, then slice the steak on the diagonal.

DRESS IT UP Place salad greens and cucumber on a serving platter. Arrange the sliced steak on the greens and sprinkle with peanuts. Drizzle the reserved dressing over the salad and serve warm.

THAI DRESSING

Place 1 cup packed coarsely chopped fresh mint or basil leaves, 1 cup prepared olive oil vinaigrette salad dressing, ⅓ cup hot cayenne pepper sauce, 3 tablespoons fresh ginger, peeled and chopped, 2 tablespoons Worcestershire sauce, 3 tablespoons sugar, and 1 tablespoon chopped garlic in a blender or food processor. Process until smooth.

Makes 6 servings

Per serving: 404 calories, 18g protein, 14g carbohydrates, 31g fat, 7g saturated fat, 29mg cholesterol, 204mg sodium

On the Menu

Enjoy all of the pleasures of the exotic cuisine of Thailand with this simple and delicious menu.

Tomato Wedges with Lemon Dressing and Cilantro

Shrimp Skewers with Spicy Peanut Sauce

Thai Beef Salad

Ginger Iced Tea

Rice Pudding with Fresh Mango

GREEK BEEF SALAD

Prep **5 MINUTES + MARINATING**   *Broil* **17 MINUTES**

Lemon Marinade (see recipe)

1 **pound beef top round steak, about 1 inch thick**

6 **cups torn romaine lettuce leaves**

1 **medium cucumber, thinly sliced**

½ **small red onion, cut into thin wedges**

2 **tablespoons crumbled feta cheese**

8 **Greek or ripe olives (optional)**

2 **pitas, toasted, cut into wedges**

What could be better than all of the glorious flavors of an authentic Greek salad turned into a satisfying main dish. For ease, the steak is broiled, but it will be even better if you grill it—don't forget the wood chips!

LET'S BEGIN Prepare the marinade. Cover and refrigerate ½ of the marinade for dressing the salad. Place the steak and the remaining marinade in a resealable plastic bag, turning the steak to coat. Press out the excess air and seal the bag. Marinate in the refrigerator for 6 hours or overnight, turning occasionally.

BROIL IT Preheat the broiler. Remove the steak from the bag (discard any marinade left in the bag) and place on a broiler pan. Broil the steak 2 to 3 inches from the heat, turning once, for 17 to 18 minutes for medium-rare steak. Let it rest for 10 minutes, then cut into thin slices.

DRESS IT UP Combine the steak slices, lettuce, cucumber, and onion in a large bowl. Add the reserved marinade and toss. Sprinkle with cheese and olives, if you wish. Serve with pita wedges.

LEMON MARINADE

Whisk together ⅔ cup fresh lemon juice, ⅓ cup olive oil, 2 teaspoons dried oregano, ½ teaspoon salt, and ½ teaspoon freshly ground black pepper in a small bowl.

Makes 4 servings

Per serving: 361 calories, 33g protein, 24g carbohydrates, 14g fat, 3g saturated fat, 76mg cholesterol, 419mg sodium

LAYERED MEXICAN SALAD

Prep **35 MINUTES**   *Broil* **7 MINUTES + STANDING**

½   cup salsa

½   cup water

2   tablespoons canola oil

2   tablespoons lime juice

1   tablespoon finely chopped cilantro

1   teaspoon sugar

1   crushed garlic clove

Roasted Bell Pepper

6   cups shredded lettuce, such as iceberg

1   medium onion, diced

1   can (12 ounces) whole kernel corn, drained

2   tomatoes, diced

½   cup shredded Cheddar cheese (2 ounces)

½   cup crushed corn chips

Using flavorful store-bought salsa as the base for the salad dressing is easy. Mild salsa is preferred, but medium adds more heat.

LET'S BEGIN Combine the first 7 ingredients in a covered container with a tight-fitting lid. Shake until well mixed, then refrigerate. Prepare the Roasted Bell Pepper.

ARRANGE Line a large serving platter with the lettuce. Layer the onion, corn, roasted pepper, and tomatoes on top. Drizzle the dressing over the salad. Top with the cheese and corn chips.

ROASTED BELL PEPPER

Place one of the oven racks 4 to 5 inches below the broiler and pre-heat the broiler. Place 1 pepper on the oven rack and broil, rotating frequently, for about 7 minutes, or until the skin blisters and turns black. Remove with tongs. Put in a paper bag to sweat for 15 minutes, or until cool enough to handle. Peel off the skin. Chop.

Makes 6 servings
Per serving: 210 calories, 6g protein, 24g carbohydrates, 12g fat, 3g saturated fat, 10mg cholesterol, 294mg sodium

---

Salad Basics

3 WAYS TO SERVE A SPEEDY LAYER SALAD

Layered salads are perfect for dinner parties and are easy to make.

- Italian-style—Start with Romaine lettuce and arugula, then add diced onion, sliced fresh mushrooms, roasted yellow pepper, diced plum tomatoes, shredded Italian fontina cheese, garlic croutons, anchovies, and a balsamic vinaigrette dressing.

- Greek-style—On a bed of fresh baby spinach, layer diced cucumbers, fava or lima beans, chopped green pepper, pitted kalamata olives, crumbled feta cheese, toasted pita crisps, and a lemon and olive oil dressing.

- Asian-style—Top a layer of shredded head lettuce with diced red pepper, bean sprouts, sliced green onions, quartered baby corn, shredded chicken or pork, chow mein noodles, and a sesame soy dressing.

SOUTH OF THE BORDER SALAD WITH HONEY JALAPEÑO DRESSING

Prep **20 MINUTES**

Honey Jalapeño Dressing (see recipe)

4 cups mixed salad greens

1 can (8 ounces) kidney beans, rinsed and drained

2 cooked boneless, skinless chicken breasts, shredded (about 1½ cups)

1 cup shredded pepper Jack cheese (4 ounces)

1 tomato, quartered

Here's the easiest way to shred semisoft cheese. Put the wrapped cheese into the freezer for about 20 minutes, or just long enough to firm it up. Then shred it with ease.

LET'S BEGIN Prepare the Honey Jalapeño Dressing and set aside.

FIX IT FAST Divide the salad greens between 2 plates. Layer each evenly with the remaining ingredients. Drizzle with the dressing.

HONEY JALAPEÑO DRESSING

Whisk together ¼ cup cider vinegar, 2 tablespoons honey, 1 table-spoon olive oil, ½ teaspoon minced garlic, and ¼ teaspoon salt in a small bowl until blended. Stir in minced fresh or canned jalapeño chile peppers to taste.

Makes 2 servings

Per serving: 650 calories, 55g protein, 45g carbohydrates, 29g fat, 14g saturated fat, 149mg cholesterol, 1,160mg sodium

CURRIED CHICKEN & SPINACH SALAD

Prep **20 MINUTES + MARINATING**   *Grill* **16 MINUTES**

Curry-Mango Chutney
  Vinaigrette (see recipe)

4   bone-in chicken breast
     halves (about 2 pounds)

12   ounces fresh spinach,
     washed and dried

3   grapefruits, peeled,
     white pith removed, and
     sectioned

4   scallions, sliced

½   cup toasted chopped
     peanuts

For the easiest and fastest way to clean fresh spinach, fill a large bowl or your sink with cool—not cold—water. Then submerge the spinach and swish it around to loosen all the grit. Lift out the spinach and drain off the water. Repeat until all the water is perfectly clean.

LET'S BEGIN Prepare the Curry-Mango Chutney Vinaigrette. Put half of the vinaigrette in a covered jar and refrigerate. Put the chicken breasts into a glass dish. Pour the remaining vinaigrette over the chicken, turning to coat all sides. Cover and refrigerate for 1 hour or up to 24 hours.

FIRE UP THE GRILL Heat the grill to medium. Transfer the chicken to the grill (discard any marinade left in the bag). Grill the chicken for 15 minutes, or until an instant-read thermometer registers 170°F when inserted into the center of the breast meat and the juices run clear. Transfer to a cutting board. Remove the skin and carefully pull the chicken off the bone in one piece. Slice each breast into a fan.

ARRANGE & SERVE Toss the spinach, grapefruit, and scallions with the vinaigrette in a bowl. Spoon onto a serving platter and arrange the chicken fans on top. Sprinkle with peanuts and serve.

CURRY-MANGO CHUTNEY VINAIGRETTE

Whisk together ⅓ cup peanut oil, ¼ cup rice vinegar, 3 tablespoons mango chutney, 1 teaspoon curry powder, ½ teaspoon salt, and ¼ teaspoon ground black pepper in a medium bowl until blended.

Makes 4 servings

Per serving: 470 calories, 41g protein, 29g carbohydrates, 22g fat, 4g saturated fat, 82mg cholesterol, 510mg sodium

SPICY THAI SHRIMP SALAD

Prep **15 MINUTES**   *Cook* **2 MINUTES**

Honey Mustard Vinaigrette
   (see recipe)

1   tablespoon vegetable oil

1½   pounds large shrimp,
       peeled and deveined

8   cups shredded Napa
       cabbage

1   red bell pepper, thinly
       sliced

1   cup thinly sliced
       cucumber

Try the English (seedless) cucumbers. They don't have to be peeled, and the seeds are so small that they don't have to be removed.

LET'S BEGIN Prepare the Honey Mustard Vinaigrette in a large bowl and set aside.

STIR-FRY Heat the oil in a large nonstick skillet or wok over medium-high heat until hot. Stir-fry the shrimp for 2 to 3 minutes, or just until they turn pink, and transfer to the bowl with the dressing. Add the cabbage, bell pepper, and cucumber, tossing to coat. Serve warm.

HONEY MUSTARD VINAIGRETTE

Combine ¾ cup prepared vinaigrette salad dressing, ¼ cup extra-hot or hot cayenne pepper sauce, ⅓ cup chopped fresh mint leaves, ¼ cup honey Dijon mustard, 1 tablespoon lime juice, and 2 teaspoons sugar substitute (sucralose) in a bowl. Whisk until well blended.

Makes 6 servings
Per serving: 292 calories, 20g protein, 13g carbohydrates, 18g fat, 3g saturated fat, 168mg cholesterol, 891mg sodium

---

Salad Basics

THE SECRET TO BUTTERFLYING SHRIMP

Butterflying shrimp is a time-honored technique that is often used in Chinese cooking. Peel the shrimp, then devein it by making a shallow cut all along the curved side of the shrimp, just deep enough to expose the dark vein. With the tip of the knife or with your fingers, remove the vein.

To butterfly the shrimp, using the same paring knife and the shallow cut you made as a guide, deepen the cut you already made, cutting almost but not all the way through,

so the shrimp is almost split in half. Whether the tail shell is left on is a matter of personal preference or the recipe you are using.

MEDITERRANEAN TUNA SALAD WITH PANCETTA VINAIGRETTE

Prep **20 MINUTES**   *Cook* **5 MINUTES**

Pancetta Vinaigrette (see recipe)

1   package (10 ounces) Italian salad greens (romaine and radicchio)

1   bunch watercress, tough stems removed

1   can (12 ounces) solid white tuna in oil, drained

1   can (19 ounces) cannelloni beans, rinsed and drained

1   jar (7 ounces) roasted red peppers, drained and sliced

½   cup chopped red onion

½   cup slivered fresh basil leaves

¼   cup capers, rinsed and drained (optional)

If you have never tried pancetta, this is the perfect opportunity. Pancetta is Italian bacon that is cured with salt and spices, but unlike American bacon, it isn't smoked. It is rolled up, somewhat resembling a large sausage. Pancetta is found in specialty and Italian food markets.

LET'S BEGIN Prepare the Pancetta Vinaigrette.

TOSS IT UP Combine the salad greens and watercress in a large bowl. Toss with just enough warm vinaigrette to coat. Divide the greens among 4 large serving plates.

DRESS IT UP Arrange the tuna in the center of each plate and surround it with the beans. Scatter the pepper strips and red onion over the beans and tuna. Sprinkle each salad with the basil and capers, if you wish. Drizzle with any remaining vinaigrette.

PANCETTA VINAIGRETTE

Cook 2 ounces diced pancetta (or bacon) over medium heat for 5 minutes or until crisp. Transfer bacon to paper towels with a slotted spoon and remove the skillet from the heat. Whisk in 1 cup prepared olive-oil-and-balsamic vinaigrette and 1 teaspoon honey into the warm skillet until blended.

Makes 4 servings
Per serving: 580 calories, 36g protein, 43g carbohydrates, 29g fat, 5g saturated fat, 53mg cholesterol, 1,501mg sodium

MEDITERRANEAN TOMATO SALAD

Prep **10 MINUTES + CHILLING**

3   pounds assorted tomatoes such as plum, yellow, or beefsteak, cut into wedges, or cherry tomatoes, halved

1   large shallot or small onion, finely chopped

¼   cup loosely packed fresh basil leaves, slivered

½   cup prepared balsamic or olive oil vinaigrette dressing

Salt and freshly ground black pepper (optional)

Parmesan cheese shavings (optional)

Head to the nearest farmers' market for the best tomatoes available. For the most interesting-looking salad, use a variety of tomatoes.

LET'S BEGIN Cut the tomatoes into wedges or halve the cherry tomatoes. Place the tomatoes in a large bowl and add the next 3 ingredients. Toss until coated.

CHILL IT Cover and refrigerate for at least 30 minutes. If you wish, just before serving, season with salt and freshly ground black pepper to taste and sprinkle with cheese shavings.

Makes 6 servings

Per serving: 106 calories, 2g protein, 12g carbohydrates, 6g fat, 1g saturated fat, 0mg cholesterol, 246mg sodium

Cook to Cook

WHAT ARE SOME THINGS TO TOSS INTO TOMATO SALADS?

"When tomatoes are in season, I like to include them in just about every meal by creatively combining them with lots of tasty ingredients. Here are some of my favorites:

I thickly *slice tomatoes and put them onto a platter along with red onion rings and lots of flat-leaf parsley* leaves. I drizzle them with any dressing I have on hand. When I have time, I make this salad an hour ahead and let it stand at room temperature. As the tomatoes stand, they soak up the dressing and their flavor intensifies and gets even better.

Sometimes I cut tomatoes into wedges and put them into a bowl with thick slices of cucumber and black olives. I *toss them with red wine vinaigrette and top off the salad with chunks of feta cheese.*

Other times I put thick wedges of tomatoes into a bowl along with torn iceberg lettuce and freshly cooked crisp bacon pieces and croutons. I drizzle it all with blue cheese dressing.

Another favorite way of mine to serve tomatoes is to *combine tomato wedges with freshly cooked corn kernels, chopped red onion, and lots of fresh cilantro.* I toss it all with lemon dressing."

MEXICAN CHOPPED SALAD

Prep **20 MINUTES**

Spicy Vinaigrette (see recipe)

6   **cups romaine lettuce leaves, torn**

1½   **cups shredded pepper Jack cheese (6 ounces)**

1   **cup peeled, diced jicama**

1   **ripe avocado, peeled, seeded, and diced**

1   **large tomato, chopped (1 cup)**

1   **cup canned black beans, rinsed and drained**

¼   **cup thinly sliced green onions**

½   **cup frozen whole kernel corn, thawed**

Jicama is sometimes called the Mexican potato. It actually resembles a large potato with its thin brown skin and pale flesh. However, jicama has a sweet, nutty flavor and is good in most salads.

LET'S BEGIN Prepare the Spicy Vinaigrette.

FIX IT FAST Combine all of the remaining ingredients in a large bowl and toss to mix.

DRESS IT UP Add the Spicy Vinaigrette and toss. To serve, arrange on 4 plates.

SPICY VINAIGRETTE

Combine ¼ cup vegetable oil, 2 tablespoons white wine vinegar, 1 minced jalapeño chile pepper, and ½ teaspoon salt in a small bowl, mixing well.

Makes 4 servings

Per serving: 453 calories, 16g protein, 26g carbohydrates, 35g fat, 11g saturated fat, 40mg cholesterol, 844mg sodium

SuperQuick
ISLAND MANGO-BERRY SALAD

Prep **25 MINUTES**

1   **pint strawberries (12 ounces), hulled and chopped**

1   **large mango, peeled, seeded, and chopped**

¼   **cup sliced green onions**

2   **tablespoons lime juice**

1   **tablespoon chopped fresh cilantro**

½   **teaspoon red-pepper flakes**

¼   **teaspoon ground cumin**

Salt (optional)

Corn chips, grilled chicken, or mild white fish (optional)

Just a little heat from red-pepper flakes adds lots of tasty interest to this simple and delicious salad.

LET'S BEGIN Put all the ingredients except the salt and corn chips in a large bowl.

TOSS & TASTE Toss the salad until well mixed. Taste and add salt, if you wish. Serve or cover and refrigerate for up to 2 days. Serve with corn chips, grilled chicken, or mild white fish, if you wish.

Makes 6 servings

Per serving: 47 calories, 1g protein, 12g carbohydrates, 0g fat, 0g saturated fat, 0mg cholesterol, 3mg sodium

---

Salad Basics

4 EASY STEPS FOR CUTTING A MANGO

A luscious tropical fruit, mango's skin color ranges from golden yellow to deeply red blushed. It is ready for eating when it yields to gentle pressure. The one drawback to this fabulous fruit is the unusually large seed that requires removal. Here are the 4 easy steps to removing the seed effortlessly.

Place the mango upright on the counter. With a serrated knife, slice through the skin and flesh, cutting down and around the seed. Repeat on the other side. You should now have 3 pieces of mango: 2 halves and the seed.

Using a paring knife, score the flesh of each mango half, cutting down (but not through) the skin.

From the skin side, push the skin to turn the mango inside out. Cut away the cubes of mango.

To remove the remaining flesh, cut around the seed. Score the strips of mango and cut to separate the flesh from the skin.

Old Bay Coleslaw, page 89

Off to the Side

This is it—the place where you'll find that old-fashioned coleslaw like Mom used to take to the church suppers, that warm potato salad that the German neighbors brought to your cookouts, and even that incredibly creamy macaroni salad that appeared every Friday in the school cafeteria. All of the salads can stand in for the vegetable course at a meal and will soon become classics your family will ask for time and again. There are a few Quick Cook tips on making salads faster than ever before. It only takes 10 minutes to create the pickled cucumber salad or the corn and tomato salad, then just chill them until suppertime. Pick out one to serve "on the side" for supper tonight.

SuperQuick
GREEN BEAN SALAD
Prep **10 MINUTES**   *Cook* **15 MINUTES**

12   ounces new red potatoes, sliced ¼-inch thick

12   ounces green beans

2   tablespoons olive oil

2   tablespoons white wine vinegar

1   tablespoon Dijon mustard

1   teaspoon garlic salt

½   teaspoon dried dill weed

½   teaspoon coarse ground black pepper

One of the greatest things about using small red potatoes is that they don't have to be peeled. Just be sure to scrub them well, preferably with a vegetable brush.

LET'S BEGIN Place the potatoes in a large saucepan or Dutch oven. Add enough water to cover by 2 inches.

BUBBLE & BOIL Cover and bring to a boil over high heat. Reduce the heat and simmer for 2 to 3 minutes. Add the green beans. Simmer 7 to 10 minutes longer, or until the vegetables are tender. Drain well and transfer to a serving bowl.

DRESS IT UP Meanwhile, whisk the remaining ingredients in a small bowl until well blended. Drizzle the dressing over the vegetables and toss gently to coat. Serve within 1 hour at room temperature or refrigerate.

Makes 6 servings

Per serving: 112 calories, 2g protein, 16g carbohydrates, 5g fat, 1g saturated fat, 0mg cholesterol, 470mg sodium

Four-Bean Salad

Prep **15 minutes + chilling**

Creole Sauce (see recipe)

1   can (16 ounces) green
    beans, drained

1   can (16 ounces) wax
    beans, drained

1   can (16 ounces) kidney
    beans, drained and
    washed

1   can (16 ounces)
    garbanzo beans, drained

1   small onion, thinly
    sliced

1   small bell pepper, thinly
    sliced

½   cup chopped green
    onions

Americans have had a love affair with two-, three-, and even four-bean salad for a long time. Part of the fun is that they are always a snap to put together, and they can be counted on to look and taste great with just about any main dish.

LET'S BEGIN Prepare the Creole Sauce and set aside.

FIX IT FAST Place the remaining ingredients in a large shallow dish and drizzle with sauce. Toss gently until well coated.

CHILL & STIR Cover and refrigerate for 24 hours, stirring occasionally. The longer this bean mixture stands, the better it tastes.

Creole Sauce

Place ¾ cup sugar (use a little less if you wish), ⅔ cup white vinegar, ½ cup vegetable oil, 1 teaspoon Creole seasoning, 1 teaspoon Louisiana-style hot sauce, and 2 tablespoons chopped parsley in a small bowl. Stir until well blended.

> **Makes 12 servings**
> *Per serving: 230 calories, 5g protein, 32g carbohydrates, 10g fat, 1g saturated fat, 0mg cholesterol, 490mg sodium*

Cajun Black-Eyed Pea & Pimiento Salad

Prep **15 MINUTES + CHILLING**

Spicy Cider Dressing (see recipe)

4 cups coarsely chopped tomatoes

½ cup chopped fresh parsley

1 can (15 ounces) black-eyed peas or black beans, rinsed and drained

1 jar (4 ounces) diced pimientos

½ cup Monterey Jack cheese, cubed (2 ounces)

6 lettuce leaves

Just the right amount of garlic and hot-pepper sauce in the dressing gives this salad that "bam" quality. If you like lots of heat, stir in additional hot sauce.

LET'S BEGIN Make the Spicy Cider Dressing.

MIX & CHILL Combine all of the remaining ingredients, except the lettuce, with the dressing in a large bowl. Mix well. Cover and refrigerate for at least 1 hour.

ARRANGE & SERVE To serve, place 1 lettuce leaf on 6 individual plates and top with the salad mixture, dividing evenly.

SPICY CIDER DRESSING

Combine 2 tablespoons cider vinegar, 1 teaspoon finely chopped fresh garlic, 1 teaspoon vegetable oil, ½ teaspoon hot-pepper sauce, ½ teaspoon sugar, and ¼ teaspoon salt in a jar with a tight-fitting lid. Shake vigorously to combine.

Makes 6 servings

Per serving: 130 calories, 7g protein, 17g carbohydrates, 4g fat, 2g saturated fat, 10mg cholesterol, 230mg sodium

Fiesta Corn Salad

Prep **10 MINUTES + CHILLING**

1   can (11 ounces) vacuum-packed whole kernel corn, drained

8   cherry tomatoes, halved

¼   cup finely chopped green onions

½   cup pepper Jack cheese, cubed (2 ounces)

1   tablespoon red wine vinegar

½   teaspoon dried oregano, crumbled

½   teaspoon ground cumin

¼   teaspoon garlic salt

If you don't have green onions on hand, you can also use chives, red onion, or even white onion. Pepper Jack cheese has an enticing amount of heat, but if you prefer, use the milder Monterey Jack cheese.

LET'S BEGIN Combine all of the ingredients in a large bowl.

CHILL Cover and refrigerate for at least 1 hour.

Makes 6 servings

Per serving: 87 calories, 4g protein, 11g carbohydrates, 3g fat, 2g saturated fat, 10mg cholesterol, 280mg sodium

Cool Cucumber Salad

Prep **10 MINUTES + CHILLING**

3   tablespoons olive oil

2   tablespoons cider vinegar

1   teaspoon sugar

½   teaspoon seasoned salt

1   large cucumber, peeled and thinly sliced

1   medium red onion, thinly sliced

Freshly ground black pepper (optional)

Serve this refreshing cucumber salad on a warm summer's day to accompany almost any grilled meat, fish, or poultry. If you like, slice the cucumber several hours ahead and store in the refrigerator in a resealable plastic bag.

LET'S BEGIN Combine the first 4 ingredients in a medium bowl. Add the cucumber and red onion. Season to taste with pepper, if you wish.

DRESS IT UP Toss the mixture to coat the vegetables well. Cover and refrigerate for up to 2 hours.

Makes 4 servings

Per serving: 109 calories, 1g protein, 5g carbohydrates, 10g fat, 1g saturated fat, 0mg cholesterol, 117mg sodium

CRIMSON SLAW

Prep **15 MINUTES + CHILLING**

Use this triply red slaw to dress up a breast of roast turkey or spiral-cut ham. Round out the meal with warm buttermilk biscuits and mashed sweet potatoes flavored with maple syrup.

Slaw Dressing (see recipe)

½ **head red cabbage, shredded**

1 **medium red onion, thinly sliced**

3 **green onions, sliced**

1 **package (6 ounces) sweetened dried cranberries**

LET'S BEGIN Prepare the Slaw Dressing.

DRESS IT UP Toss all of the remaining ingredients in a large bowl. Add the dressing and toss until well coated.

CHILL Cover the slaw and refrigerate for 1 hour or up to 6 hours. Stir before serving.

SLAW DRESSING

Whisk 6 tablespoons olive oil, 2 tablespoons red wine vinegar, 2 tablespoons sugar, 1 teaspoon salt, ½ teaspoon ground black pepper, ½ teaspoon cumin, and ¼ teaspoon ground mustard in a small bowl until well blended.

Makes 6 servings
Per serving: 237 calories, 1g protein, 29g carbohydrates, 14g fat, 2g saturated fat, 0mg cholesterol, 396mg sodium

Food Facts

THE KOOLSLA OF COLESLAW

In the Dutch language, *koolsla* stands for cabbage salad—derived from *kool* meaning cabbage and *sla*, salad. The connection of the name with the temperature cold is unclear, though its name is often mistaken for the name *cold slaw*.

Whatever the spelling and origin of the dish, coleslaw is clearly an important part of any salad bar. Today, it comes mixed with a mayonnaise or tossed with a vinaigrette dressing. It may or may not contain other shredded vegetables such as carrots and bell peppers.

COUNTRY COLESLAW

Prep **15 MINUTES + CHILLING**

Country Dressing (see recipe)

5   cups shredded cabbage

1   cup shredded carrots

½   cup diced red bell pepper

½   cup diced green bell pepper

½   cup chopped green onion

½   cup chopped fresh parsley (optional)

Make this slaw ahead so that at serving time all you have to do is toss it. Shred, chop, or dice the vegetables, and refrigerate in a covered bowl. Then prepare the dressing, cover, and refrigerate. How easy is that?

LET'S BEGIN Prepare Country Dressing.

DRESS IT UP Toss all of the remaining ingredients in a large bowl, including the parsley if you wish. Add the dressing and toss until well coated. Cover the coleslaw and refrigerate for at least 1 hour before serving.

COUNTRY DRESSING

Combine 1 cup mayonnaise, 3 tablespoons cider vinegar, 2 table-spoons sugar, 1½ teaspoons salt, and ¼ teaspoon red-pepper sauce in a small bowl.

Makes 6 servings

Per serving: 200 calories, 2g protein, 20g carbohydrates, 13g fat, 2g saturated fat, 10mg cholesterol, 885mg sodium

---

Time Savers

5 RULES FOR MAKING SWIFTER SALADS

Dinner in most homes means "a vegetable salad on the side." But all that crisping and peeling and slicing and dicing take time. Here are some strategies that will speed up the process.

- **PLAN AHEAD:** Rinse and spin-dry lettuces for several nights at once. Wrap them in paper towels and refrigerate them in a plastic bag. You can even tear and tightly wrap greens right in the salad bowl, then refrigerate overnight.

- **GET OUTSIDE HELP:** Select salad-ready vegetables from your supermarket's produce section or salad bar; crumbled or shredded cheeses from the dairy section; and canned, marinated, or pickled vegetables for jiffy toppings.

- **GET INSIDE HELP:** Enlist the kids. Rinsing vegetables, using a salad spinner, and tear-

ing up lettuce is safe for little fingers and lots of fun.

- **DOUBLE UP:** Cook twice as many vegetables as you need for supper one night and you'll have precooked toppings for your salad the next.

- **JUMP-START THE FLAVOR:** Marinate sliced tomatoes, onions, and carrots in dressing overnight. They'll deliver much more flavor to the salad bowl the next day.

OLD BAY COLESLAW

Prep **15 MINUTES + CHILLING**

1	cup mayonnaise
2	tablespoons vinegar
2	tablespoons sugar
2½	to 3 teaspoons Old Bay Seasoning
7	cups shredded cabbage
1	cup shredded carrots

Shred the cabbage and carrots up to a day ahead and store them in a large resealable plastic bag in the refrigerator. Then all of the "hard" work for this flavorful slaw is done.

FIX IT FAST In a large bowl, blend the mayonnaise, vinegar, sugar, and seasoning. Mix in the cabbage and carrots.

LET IT CHILL Cover and refrigerate for 2 hours, or until ready to serve. Stir the coleslaw and sprinkle it with extra seasoning before serving, if you wish.

Makes 8 servings

Per serving: 147 calories, 1g protein, 15g carbohydrates, 10g fat, 1g saturated fat, 8mg cholesterol, 436mg sodium

WARM RED CABBAGE & BACON

Prep **30 MINUTES**   *Cook* **8 MINUTES**

3   slices reduced-fat turkey bacon

1½   tablespoons olive oil

1   medium onion, chopped

3   large ribs celery, sliced

⅓   cup cider vinegar

3   tablespoons sugar

½   teaspoon celery seed

6   cups shredded red cabbage

Salt and freshly ground black pepper (optional)

2   tablespoons chopped fresh parsley

The red vinegar ensures that the red cabbage keeps its color and doesn't turn bluish when cooked.

LET'S BEGIN Cut the bacon into 1-inch pieces. Sauté over medium-low heat in a very large, deep skillet until it is crisp. Remove bacon to paper towels with a slotted spoon. Discard any fat left in the skillet.

INTO THE SKILLET Pour the olive oil into the skillet and place it over high heat. Sauté the onion and celery for 2 minutes.

BUBBLE & BOIL Add the vinegar, sugar, and celery seed and bring to a boil, then immediately add the cabbage and bacon pieces. Stir and toss for about 1 minute, or until the cabbage is warm, but not cooked. Season to taste with salt and pepper, if you wish, and sprinkle with parsley. Serve right away.

Makes 4 servings

Per serving: 190 calories, 6g protein, 22g carbohydrates, 7g fat, 2g saturated fat, 15mg cholesterol, 300mg sodium

---

Salad Basics

GREAT POTATO SALAD 1-2-3

Make any meal better with a potato salad! Put together this ever-favorite dish with ease:

CHOOSE SMART The key to success is choosing the right potato. The all-time best potatoes for salads are low-starch or waxy potatoes. Some popular types are Red Bliss and Yellow Fin. All-purpose potatoes, such as Yukon Gold, are fine for salads, but their texture is a bit softer.

COOK IT RIGHT Did you know that there is a correct way to cook potatoes? Put the potatoes, peeled or unpeeled, into a saucepan filled with enough salted water to cover and bring it to a boil. Reduce the heat and simmer just until the potatoes are tender. Immediately pour the potatoes and water into a colander to drain well.

SALAD TIME When the potatoes are cool enough to handle, cut them into chunks and put them into a bowl. Add the extra ingredients to the potatoes while they are still warm so they can absorb all of the flavors. If you are not serving the salad for several hours, cover the bowl with plastic wrap and refrigerate. Then take the potato salad out of the fridge about 30 minutes before serving to take off the chill. Be sure to give the salad a taste and season additionally with salt and pepper, if needed.

RED-SKIN POTATO SALAD WITH HONEY DILL DRESSING

Prep **25 MINUTES**   *Cook* **20 MINUTES**

1½   **pounds small red new potatoes**

4   **slices bacon**

1   **medium onion, diced**

6   **tablespoons honey**

6   **tablespoons apple cider vinegar**

½   **teaspoon cornstarch mixed with ½ teaspoon water**

2   **tablespoons chopped fresh dill or 1 tablespoon dried dill weed**

1   **bunch watercress, washed and chopped**

Here is a tip for the quickest way to trim and wash watercress. Trim the tough stems by cutting through the bunch just above the rubber band that holds it together. Then swish the watercress sprigs in a large bowl of cold water until well rinsed. Shake or spin it dry, and you're good to go.

LET'S BEGIN Put the potatoes in a large saucepan and cover with water. Add salt if you wish. Bring to a boil over high heat. Reduce the heat to medium and cook for 12 minutes or until tender but still firm. Drain and let cool. Meanwhile, sauté the bacon in a large skillet until crisp. Transfer the bacon to paper towels to drain (do not discard the drippings). When cool, crumble the bacon.

COOK IT UP Add the onion to the bacon drippings in the skillet and cook for 3 minutes, or until soft. Add the honey and vinegar, stirring to combine. Bring to a boil. Stir in the cornstarch mixture and cook until thickened. Remove from the heat. Stir in the crumbled bacon and dill.

DRESS IT UP Halve the potatoes (leave the skins on) and toss with the watercress in a large bowl. Drizzle on the dressing and toss gently. Serve.

Makes 6 servings

Per serving: 224 calories, 5g protein, 36g carbohydrates, 6g fat, 2g saturated fat, 11mg cholesterol, 211mg sodium

FRENCH POTATO SALAD

Prep **20 MINUTES**   *Cook* **15 MINUTES**

Dijon-Tarragon Dressing (see recipe)

1⅓ pounds red-skinned potatoes, cut into bite-size chunks

1   cup sliced celery

2   hard-cooked eggs, coarsely chopped

2   tablespoons drained capers

¾   teaspoon salt

Freshly ground black pepper (optional)

Lettuce leaves (optional)

Tossing still-warm potatoes with dressing is a classic French technique that is very smart. The potatoes soak up the dressing, making them tasty through and through.

LET'S BEGIN Prepare the Dijon-Tarragon Dressing. Put the potatoes into a medium saucepan and cover with water. Bring to a boil over high heat. Reduce the heat to medium, cover, and cook for 10 to 12 minutes, or until just tender when pierced with a fork. Drain.

DRESS IT UP Add the warm potatoes to the dressing and toss to coat. Add the celery, eggs, capers, and salt, tossing gently to combine. Season to taste with pepper and serve on 4 lettuce-lined salad plates, if you wish.

DIJON-TARRAGON DRESSING

Whisk together ⅓ cup olive oil, 3 tablespoons Dijon mustard, 3 tablespoons white wine vinegar, 1 finely chopped garlic clove, and ½ teaspoon dried tarragon leaves in a bowl until well blended.

> **Makes 4 servings**
>
> Per serving: 325 calories, 9g protein, 27g carbohydrates, 21g fat, 3g saturated fat, 106mg cholesterol, 890mg sodium

---

Cooking Basics

FRESH WAYS WITH POTATO SALADS

Ever since the potato salad became popular in the mid-nineteenth century, folks have spent years creating their own signature version. Here are some to try the next time potato salad is on the menu.

- **SPINACH SPECIAL:** Toss cooked potatoes with fresh baby spinach, crumbled bacon, and hot bacon dressing.
- **SCANDINAVIAN:** Combine cooked red potatoes with a jar of herring and some chopped fresh dill. The

sauce that comes with the herring is usually enough to dress 4 servings.

- **PACIFIC NORTHWEST:** Mix white wine vinaigrette with chopped sweet onions and fresh berries to cooked, halved fingerling potatoes.

ALL-AMERICAN POTATO SALAD

Prep **25 MINUTES**   *Cook* **15 MINUTES + CHILLING**

1⅓   pounds potatoes
      (4 medium)

2   teaspoons salt

Sour Cream Dressing (see
recipe)

2   ounces bacon, cooked
      and crumbled

2   hard-cooked eggs,
      coarsely chopped

2   ounces blue cheese,
      crumbled

The fabulous Sour Cream Dressing is also delicious tossed with cooked macaroni, spooned over a crisp green salad, or served alongside celery sticks for an easy appetizer.

LET'S BEGIN Peel the potatoes and cut them into 1-inch chunks. In a large saucepan, combine the potatoes, salt, and enough water to cover. Bring to a boil over high heat. Reduce the heat to medium, cover, and cook 12 to 15 minutes, or until the potatoes are tender when pierced with a fork. Transfer to a large bowl.

DRESS IT UP Meanwhile, prepare the Sour Cream Dressing. Spoon over the potatoes and add the remaining ingredients. Toss until well coated and season with additional salt, if you wish.

CHILL Cover and refrigerate for several hours.

SOUR CREAM DRESSING

Combine 1 cup low-fat sour cream, ½ cup lowfat mayonnaise, 1 tablespoon Dijon mustard, ½ teaspoon finely chopped garlic, ¼ teaspoon cayenne pepper, and ⅛ to ¼ teaspoon white pepper in a blender. Process until well blended.

> ### Makes 6 servings
> *Per serving: 283 calories, 12g protein, 20g carbohydrates, 18g fat, 10g saturated fat, 106mg cholesterol, 526mg sodium*

SuperQuick

EASY HOT GERMAN POTATO SALAD

Prep **5 MINUTES** *Cook* **20 MINUTES**

2	tablespoons butter
1	pound round white potatoes, cut into ¾-inch pieces
1½	cups sliced celery
⅓	cup real bacon bits
	Hot Vinegar Dressing (see recipe)
¼	cup chopped fresh parsley
2	hard-cooked eggs, chopped

Use peeled or unpeeled potatoes with equal success. Just be sure to scrub the skins well.

LET'S BEGIN Melt the butter in a 10-inch skillet over medium heat until sizzling, then add the potatoes. Cook, stirring occasionally, for 20 to 25 minutes, or until golden brown and tender.

TOSS Transfer the potatoes to a large bowl and toss with the celery and bacon. Set aside and keep warm.

DRESS IT UP Meanwhile, prepare the Hot Vinegar Dressing. Pour the dressing over the potato mixture and toss to coat. Divide the potato salad among 4 individual serving plates. Sprinkle with parsley and chopped egg.

HOT VINEGAR DRESSING

Melt 1 tablespoon butter in a skillet until sizzling and add ¾ cup chopped onion. Cook over medium heat until onion is softened (1 to 2 minutes). Combine 1 tablespoon flour, 1 tablespoon sugar, 1 teaspoon dry mustard, ½ teaspoon salt, and ¼ teaspoon freshly ground black pepper in a small bowl. Stir the flour mixture into the onion mixture. Stir in ⅔ cup water and ¼ cup cider vinegar. Continue cooking, stirring constantly, until mixture comes to a boil (2 to 3 minutes). Continue cooking 1 minute.

> ### Makes 4 servings
> *Per serving: 280 calories, 10g protein, 31g carbohydrates, 13g fat, 6g saturated fat, 135mg cholesterol, 730mg sodium*

Sour Cream Dill Potato Salad

Prep **30 MINUTES**   *Cook* **12 MINUTES + CHILLING**

6   cups water

1   teaspoon salt

3   pounds small new red potatoes, scrubbed and quartered

Creamy Dressing (see recipe)

5   slices crisp-cooked bacon, crumbled

2   hard-cooked eggs, sliced

2   tablespoons thinly sliced green onions

For perfect hard-cooked eggs, put the eggs into a saucepan with enough water to cover by 1 inch and bring to a boil. Remove from the heat, cover, and let rest for 12 minutes. Then drain and run the eggs under cold water.

LET'S BEGIN Bring water and salt to a full boil in a large saucepan or Dutch oven over high heat. Add the potatoes. Reduce the heat to medium and cook until the potatoes are fork tender, about 12 to 15 minutes. Rinse with cold water, drain, and place in a large bowl.

DRESS IT UP Prepare the Creamy Dressing. Pour over the potatoes and stir gently to combine. Top the salad with bacon, egg slices, and onions.

CHILL Cover the salad. Refrigerate for 4 hours or overnight to blend the flavors before serving.

CREAMY DRESSING

Stir together ½ cup sour cream, ½ cup mayonnaise, ¼ cup chopped fresh parsley, 1½ cups sliced celery, 1 tablespoon chopped fresh dill (or ½ teaspoon dried dill weed), 1 tablespoon Dijon mustard, 1 teaspoon finely chopped fresh garlic, ½ teaspoon salt, and ¼ teaspoon freshly ground black pepper in a medium bowl.

Makes 10 servings

Per serving: 250 calories, 6g protein, 26g carbohydrates, 14g fat, 4g saturated fat, 55mg cholesterol, 550mg sodium

COUNTRY MACARONI SALAD

Prep **10 MINUTES**   *Cook* **15 MINUTES + CHILLING**

8   ounces elbow macaroni

Dijon Mayonnaise (see recipe)

1   cup chopped red, yellow, and orange bell peppers

½   cup chopped green onions

1   cup sliced celery

Macaroni salad has been popular in the South since the 1950s, especially in school cafeterias. The recipes always varied, but one could always count on lots of creamy mayonnaise.

LET'S BEGIN Prepare the macaroni according to package directions. Rinse and drain.

DRESS IT UP Meanwhile, prepare the Dijon Mayonnaise. Gently stir in the macaroni and the remaining ingredients until well mixed.

CHILL Cover and refrigerate for 1 hour, or until thoroughly chilled.

DIJON MAYONNAISE

Combine 1 cup mayonnaise, 2 tablespoons white wine vinegar, 1 tablespoon Dijon mustard, 2 teaspoons granulated sugar, 1½ teaspoons salt, and ¼ teaspoon freshly ground black pepper in a large bowl.

Makes 8 servings
Per serving: 245 calories, 5g protein, 34g carbohydrates, 10g fat, 2g saturated fat, 8mg cholesterol, 706mg sodium

SuperQuick
PASTA SALAD

Prep **10 MINUTES**   *Cook* **15 MINUTES**

8   ounces pasta (such as
     penne, farfalle, or
     rotini)

Basil Dressing (see recipe)

6   tomatoes, sliced into
     wedges

½   cup shredded mozzarella
     cheese or crumbled light
     feta cheese

The ever-popular salad combination of tomatoes, basil, and mozzarella gets even better when combined with cooked pasta. The dressing is so lovely, you will want to spoon it over cooked green beans, grilled shrimp, or cooked carrots.

LET'S BEGIN Cook the pasta according to package directions. Drain well and transfer to a large bowl. Meanwhile, prepare the Basil Dressing.

DRESS IT UP Add the tomatoes and cheese to the pasta and stir to mix. Drizzle with the dressing and toss to coat. Adjust the seasonings before serving, if you wish. This salad is best when served at room temperature. To store leftover salad, cover and refrigerate, then let warm to room temperature to serve.

BASIL DRESSING

Combine ¼ cup canola oil, 1 minced garlic clove, ¼ cup shredded fresh basil leaves, and salt and freshly ground black pepper to taste in a small bowl.

Makes 8 servings

Per serving: 195 calories, 6g protein, 23g carbohydrates, 9g fat, 1g saturated fat, 5mg cholesterol, 85mg sodium

ZESTY SUMMER PASTA SALAD

Prep **5 MINUTES**   *Cook* **10 MINUTES + CHILLING**

6   ounces dried angel hair pasta, broken into thirds

¾   cup fat-free Italian dressing

¼   cup sliced ripe olives

¼   cup pepperoni slices (about 1½ ounces)

¼   cup chopped fresh basil leaves

8   ounce slice (1-inch thick) deli reduced-fat mozzarella cheese, cut into ½-inch cubes

2   large tomatoes, cut into 1-inch chunks

1   medium green bell pepper, chopped

The only time it is okay to rinse cooked pasta is when putting it into a pasta salad. Rinsing off the excess starch ensures that the pasta won't clump up. If you want to cook the pasta up to 4 hours ahead, toss it with a little bit of oil and store it in the refrigerator.

LET'S BEGIN Cook the pasta according to the package directions. Rinse with cold water and drain. Transfer the pasta to a large bowl.

DRESS IT UP Add all of the remaining ingredients to the bowl and toss to coat well. Cover and refrigerate for at least 2 hours before serving.

Makes 8 servings

Per serving: 180 calories, 14g protein, 18g carbohydrates, 6g fat, 3g saturated fat, 10mg cholesterol, 800mg sodium

CARROT RAISIN RICE SALAD

Prep **20 MINUTES**   *Cook* **20 MINUTES + CHILLING**

Creamy Dressing (see recipe)

12 cups cooked and cooled converted rice

12 cups coarsely shredded carrots

3   cups diced celery

4   cups raisins

¾   cup thinly sliced green onion

Carrot and raisin salads have always been popular, especially in school cafeterias and luncheonettes. Combining it with cooked rice makes it an outstanding side dish.

LET'S BEGIN Prepare the Creamy Dressing and set aside.

DRESS IT UP Combine the remaining ingredients in a very large bowl. Pour the dressing over the rice mixture. Toss well and refrigerate until serving.

CREAMY DRESSING

Combine 3 cups mayonnaise, 1½ cups sour cream, ½ cup water, ⅓ cup white vinegar, ¼ cup sugar, and 4 tablespoons lemon juice in a medium bowl.

Makes 25 servings

Per serving: 333 calories, 4g protein, 54g carbohydrates, 12g fat, 3g saturated fat, 12mg cholesterol, 260mg sodium

---

Cook to Cook

WHAT'S YOUR SECRET FOR SPICING UP RICE SALADS?

❝I love versatile and flavorful rice salads because there are so many different things you can do to make them different and interesting. Here are a couple of my favorite ways *to spark a bowl of freshly cooked white or brown rice for four.*

If the rice salad is a side dish, allow ½ cup cooked rice per person; if the salad is for a main course, allow 1 cup cooked rice per person.

I sometimes *like to make a mixed seafood and rice salad.*

To my bowl of rice, I add some cooked shrimp and mussels or clams, some chopped fresh tomato and parsley along with some celery (for crunch). I dress it with a basic lemon vinaigrette with some garlic and freshly grated lemon zest tossed in.

To curry up a rice salad, I add some curry powder to ranch-style dressing and toss in some coarsely chopped apple, dark raisins, and cubed cooked chicken or turkey. Once the ingredients are nicely mixed, I top it all off with

toasted grated coconut, sliced or slivered almonds, and a bit of chopped cilantro. Fabulous!

Another favorite way with rice salad is the fruit approach. To a bowl of rice, I add drained mandarin orange segments, some chopped dates, golden raisins, and some thinly sliced radishes. To a basic vinaigrette, I add some ground cinnamon and cumin, as well as a nice pinch of cayenne.❞

TOMATO & BULGUR SALAD

Prep **15 MINUTES + STANDING**

Bulgur wheat is a nutritious staple enjoyed in the Middle East. It is made from wheat kernels that have been steamed, dried, and crushed. It has a tempting chewy texture and is available in fine, medium, and coarse grinds. The best part is that it doesn't get cooked: It is softened in boiling water.

½	cup bulgur (uncooked)
1	cup boiling water
2	medium tomatoes, cut into ½-inch cubes
½	cup chopped mild onion
¼	cup chopped fresh parsley
¼	cup homemade or prepared Italian salad dressing
2	teaspoons minced garlic
½	teaspoon salt
¼	to ½ teaspoon ground coriander (optional)

LET'S BEGIN Place the bulgur in a medium, heatproof bowl. Pour the boiling water over it and let stand until the bulgur is softened, about 15 minutes. Drain and return the bulgur to the bowl.

DRESS IT UP Stir in the remaining ingredients. Toss to mix. Serve immediately or cover and refrigerate for up to 2 days.

Makes 4 servings

Per serving: 130 calories, 3g protein, 20g carbohydrates, 5g fat, 1g saturated fat, 0mg cholesterol, 543mg sodium

Moroccan Fruit Salad

Prep **45 minutes**

Citrus Dressing (see recipe)

1 large banana, sliced

3 cups cooked couscous, cooled

½ cup chopped red apple

⅓ cup sliced celery

¼ cup chopped walnuts, toasted

North Africans have a knack for creating the most exotic-tasting salads from common ingredients, and this one is no exception. Don't even think of leaving out the ground cinnamon—it's what makes the dressing special.

LET'S BEGIN Prepare the Citrus Dressing.

DRESS IT UP Combine the remaining ingredients in a large bowl. Pour the dressing over the salad and toss to evenly coat.

Citrus Dressing

Stir together ½ cup plus 2 tablespoons orange juice, 3 tablespoons olive oil, 1 tablespoon lemon juice, ½ teaspoon salt, and ⅛ teaspoon ground cinnamon in a small bowl.

Makes 4 servings

Per serving: 325 calories, 7g protein, 42g carbohydrates, 15g fat, 2g saturated fat, 0mg cholesterol, 306mg sodium

Market Salad

Prep **15 MINUTES + CHILLING**

Herb Vinaigrette (see recipe)

2   **cups small cauliflower florets**

2   **cups small broccoli florets**

2   **medium carrots, cut into matchstick strips**

1   **can (15 ounces) garbanzo beans, rinsed and drained**

¾   **cup chopped red bell pepper**

2   **cups shredded mozzarella cheese (8 ounces)**

To save time in the kitchen, purchase packaged cauliflower and broccoli florets, which are found in the produce section of supermarkets and specialty food stores.

LET'S BEGIN Prepare the Herb Vinaigrette.

DRESS IT UP Combine the remaining ingredients in a large bowl. Add the vinaigrette and toss gently.

CHILL Cover the bowl and refrigerate for 30 minutes. Stir gently before serving.

Herb Vinaigrette

Combine ⅓ cup white wine vinegar, 2 minced garlic cloves, 1 teaspoon dried oregano, and ¼ teaspoon salt in a small bowl. Whisk in ½ cup vegetable oil slowly until the mixture is smooth and thickened. Stir in 2 teaspoons capers, if you wish.

> *Makes 8 servings*
>
> *Per serving: 321 calories, 13g protein, 22g carbohydrates, 21g fat, 6g saturated fat, 17mg cholesterol, 420mg sodium*

Fresh Fruit Parfait Mold, page 110

The Fruit Basket

Remember those shimmering gelatin fruit salads that Mother used to make every Sunday? Well, here are a few of the very best—a towering, luscious, layered orange and pineapple mold and a creamy ambrosia reminiscent of many dinner parties down South. And in case you've never had much luck with unmolding these, there are tips included for ensuring your creation comes out perfectly every time. But that's not all! There are fruit salads made with fresh berries for summer, another with apples and dried fruits for the fall. An anytime recipe lets you pick an assortment of the best fruit in the marketplace and drizzle it with a scrumptious homemade poppy seed dressing. Divine! Whatever the season, these fruits salads deliver pure refreshment.

LIGHT & FRUITY RASPBERRY MOLD

Prep **15 MINUTES**   *Microwave* **1 MINUTE + CHILLING**

1   bottle (48 ounces or 6 cups) light cranberry-raspberry juice drink

4   envelopes unflavored gelatin

1   package (0.3 ounce) raspberry sugar-free gelatin

1   can (20 ounces) crushed pineapple, drained

1   can (10 ounces) mandarin oranges, drained

1   cup seedless green grapes, halved

Enjoy slices of this bejeweled fruit mold after a hearty main dish or to end a lunch with friends. Softly whipped cream, served alongside, will add just the right touch of richness.

LET'S BEGIN Lightly coat a mold or Bundt pan with nonstick cooking spray. Pour 1½ cups of the cranberry-raspberry juice drink into a large glass mixing bowl. Sprinkle the gelatins over the juice drink, and let it sit for about 2 minutes to allow the gelatin to soften.

COOK IT FAST Microwave the gelatin mixture on High for 1 minute, or until warm. Don't let it boil. Remove from the microwave and stir until the gelatin is completely dissolved. Stir in the remaining juice.

CHILL & UNMOLD Place in the refrigerator until the mixture begins to thicken. Stir in the remaining ingredients. Pour into the mold or Bundt pan. Refrigerate until set, 8 to 12 hours. Unmold to serve. Store in the refrigerator.

Makes 12 servings

Per serving: 72 calories, 1g protein, 18g carbohydrates, 0g fat, 0g saturated fat, 0mg cholesterol, 57mg sodium

LAYERED ORANGE PINEAPPLE MOLD

Prep **20 MINUTES + CHILLING**

1   can (20 ounces) crushed
     pineapple in juice,
     undrained

Cold water

1½   cups boiling water

1   package (8-serving size)
     orange flavor gelatin

1   package (8 ounces)
     cream cheese, softened

This simple and delicious molded salad can be garnished many ways: Surround it with fresh mint sprigs, small whole strawberries, or segments of fresh orange.

LET'S BEGIN Coat a 6-cup mold with nonstick cooking spray. Drain the pineapple, reserving the juice in a liquid measuring cup. Add enough cold water to the juice to measure 1½ cups. Stir the boiling water into the gelatin in a large bowl for 2 minutes, or until completely dissolved. Stir in the pineapple juice mixture. Set aside 1 cup gelatin at room temperature.

STIR IT UP Stir half of the crushed pineapple into the remaining gelatin in the bowl and pour into the prepared mold. Refrigerate for about 2 hours, or until set but not firm (it should stick to a finger when touched and should mound when lifted with a spoon).

CHILL & UNMOLD Stir the reserved 1 cup gelatin gradually into the cream cheese in a medium bowl, with a wire whisk, until smooth. Stir in the remaining crushed pineapple and pour over the gelatin layer in the mold. Refrigerate for 4 hours, or until firm. Unmold to serve. Store in the refrigerator.

Makes 12 servings

Per serving: 150 calories, 7g protein, 21g carbohydrates, 7g fat, 4g saturated fat, 20mg cholesterol, 130mg sodium

Salad Basics

THE EASY WAY TO UNMOLD GELATIN SALAD

Molded gelatin desserts are fun because they can be made into many beautiful shapes and colors. Once your dessert is in its mold, the hard part is over.

All that is left now is allowing the gelatin to set up. Keep in mind that small gelatin molds take a

good 4 hours to set up, while large molds should be refrigerated for at least 8 hours.

Follow these easy steps to get your molded creation to the table:

1. To loosen gelatin from its mold, lower the mold into a large bowl of hot (tap) water.

2. Dip the molds for 3 to 10 seconds in the hot water.

3. Next, invert a plate on top of the mold and turn the mold and plate over together.

4. Now, carefully lift off the mold, and enjoy the compliments!

Fresh Fruit Parfait Mold

Prep **20 MINUTES + CHILLING**

1½ cups boiling water

1 package (8-serving size) strawberry flavor sugar-free low-calorie gelatin

1½ cups cold water

¾ cup blueberries

¾ cup hulled, chopped strawberries

1½ cups thawed light whipped topping

The great thing about gelatin molds is that they can be prepared up to a day ahead. All you have to do is unmold them and wait for the accolades. Garnish them with blueberries and strawberries to accentuate their flavors.

LET'S BEGIN Coat a 6-cup mold with cooking spray. Stir the boiling water into the gelatin in a large bowl for 2 minutes, or until completely dissolved. Stir in the cold water. Refrigerate for about 1¼ hours, or until slightly thickened (the consistency of unbeaten egg whites).

STIR IT UP Reserve 1½ cups gelatin at room temperature. Stir the fruit into the remaining gelatin in the bowl and spoon into the prepared 6-cup mold. Refrigerate for 15 minutes, or until set but not firm (it should stick to the finger when touched and should mound when lifted with a spoon).

CHILL & UNMOLD Stir the whipped topping into the reserved gelatin with a wire whisk until smooth. Spoon the mixture over the gelatin in the mold. Refrigerate for 4 hours, or until firm. Unmold to serve. Store in the refrigerator.

Makes 12 servings

Per serving: 70 calories, 1g protein, 9g carbohydrates, 4g fat, 3g saturated fat, 0mg cholesterol, 45mg sodium

CREAMY FRUITED MOLD

Prep **15 MINUTES + CHILLING**

The best way to be assured that gelatin is dissolved is to rub a small portion between your fingers to be sure you can't feel it. Use fresh seasonal fruit as any will be fabulous here.

1   cup boiling water

1   package (4-serving size) flavored gelatin of your choice

¾   cup cold water

1½ cups thawed whipped topping

1   cup diced fruit

Fresh fruit and mint leaves (optional)

LET'S BEGIN Coat a 5-cup mold with cooking spray. Stir the boiling water into the gelatin in a large bowl for 2 minutes, or until completely dissolved. Stir in the cold water. Refrigerate for about 1¼ hours, or until slightly thickened (the consistency of unbeaten egg whites).

STIR IT UP Add the whipped topping to the gelatin mixture, stirring gently until well blended. Refrigerate about 15 minutes, or until slightly thickened (a spoon drawn through will leave a definite impression). Stir in the fruit.

CHILL & UNMOLD Pour into the prepared mold. Refrigerate for 4 hours, or until firm. Unmold and garnish with additional fresh fruit and mint leaves, if you wish. Store in the refrigerator.

Makes 8 servings

Per serving: 80 calories, 1g protein, 15g carbohydrates, 3g fat, 3g saturated fat, 0mg cholesterol, 55mg sodium

Microwave in Minutes

A FOOLPROOF METHOD FOR MELTING GELATIN

When making gelatin desserts, melting the gelatin completely is very important. Using your microwave is the fastest and neatest way:

1. Sprinkle the gelatin over the specified amount of water in a custard cup and let it stand for about 5 minutes to soften.
2. Now, microwave the gelatin mixture on Low or Medium-Low at 5-second intervals, stirring after each 5 seconds, just until the water is warm (not hot) and the gelatin has dissolved.
3. For a quick test to see if it's completely melted, rub a bit of the mixture between your fingers.

GRANDMA'S FROZEN SALAD

Prep **15 MINUTES + STANDING + FREEZING**

1   **can (20 ounces) crushed pineapple**

2   **cups miniature marshmallows**

1   **package (8 ounces) cream cheese, softened**

½   **cup mayonnaise**

2   **medium bananas, sliced**

½   **cup quartered maraschino cherries**

¼   **cup chopped candied ginger (optional)**

1   **cup heavy cream, whipped**

This easy and tasty frozen molded salad makes a great accompaniment to grilled meat, but it's also good for dessert because it is so refreshing and the marshmallows make it fun to eat.

LET'S BEGIN Combine the undrained pineapple and marshmallows in a bowl. Cover and let stand 3 to 4 hours, until most of the syrup is absorbed.

FOLD IT IN Beat the cream cheese with the mayonnaise in a large bowl. Beat in the pineapple mixture. Fold in the bananas, cherries, and ginger, if you wish. Carefully fold in the whipped cream.

FREEZE & UNMOLD Pour into a 2-quart ring mold or two 8½ × 4½-inch loaf pans. Freeze for 8 hours, or until firm. Unmold and cut in slices to serve.

Makes 8 servings

Per serving: 433 calories, 3g protein, 34g carbohydrates, 32g fat, 15g saturated fat, 77mg cholesterol, 199mg sodium

---

Cook to Cook

WHERE CAN I GET THOSE FANCY FLOWERS TO GARNISH A SPECIAL DISH?

"Many flowers are edible and safe to use as food decorations and garnishes. They're *great for tossing into the salad bowl, decorating an arranged salad,* or for garnishing a salad mold.

Look for flowers grown by spe- cialty produce growers that deliver *pesticide-free edible blossoms.* I buy them at my local farmer's market and often can find them at gourmet grocery stores. Avoid buying them at a florist or a nursery.

There are two kinds of edible blossoms—flowers that are grown specifically for eating, such as *pansies, and flowers that come from the vegetable growers,* such as squash blossoms. "

AMBROSIA WITH HONEY LIME CREAM
Prep **30 MINUTES**

Honey Lime Cream Dressing (see recipe)

¼ cup honey

2 tablespoons lime juice

3 oranges, peeled and sliced

2 bananas, peeled and sliced

1 red apple, cored and cubed

1 green apple, cored and cubed

1 cup sweetened flaked coconut

This ambrosia is also luscious spooned over thick wedges of angel food cake or coconut pound cake. We even like it served over slices of toasted plain pound cake.

LET'S BEGIN Prepare the Honey Lime Cream Dressing and set aside.

DRESS IT UP Combine the honey and lime juice in a large bowl. Add the next 4 ingredients and toss.

LAYER & TOP Layer the fruit alternately with the coconut in a serving bowl. Top with Honey Lime Cream Dressing. Refrigerate covered until serving.

HONEY LIME CREAM DRESSING

Beat ½ cup heavy cream in a medium bowl until fluffy. Drizzle in 2 tablespoons honey and beat until stiff. Fold in 1 teaspoon grated lime zest.

Makes 4 servings

Per serving: 476 calories, 4g protein, 74g carbohydrates, 22g fat, 17g saturated fat, 41mg cholesterol, 104mg sodium

---

Food Facts

THE SOUTH'S LOVE WITH AMBROSIA

The word *ambrosia* (meaning "immortality") dates back to classical Greek mythology, where it was the food of the gods on Mount Olympus. Take a bite of the dessert, now known by the same name, and you can understand why. It's a heavenly sweet creation that dates back at least to the 19th century in America and was an especially popular, elegant dessert served on the Southern plantations. In those days, ambrosia was made by alternating layers of circular slices of fresh oranges, thin slices of fresh pineapple, freshly grated coconut, and sifted loaf sugar.

Ambrosia still typically contains fresh oranges, pineapple, and sugar—but now often appears also with bananas, mini marshmallows, and chunks of crisp apples. The ingredients are carefully layered, then the whole dessert is chilled. As ambrosia chills, some of the mini marshmallows dissolve, making the dessert even sweeter and more heavenly!

AMBROSIA MOLD

Prep **15 MINUTES + CHILLING**

1   can (8 ounces) crushed
    pineapple in juice,
    undrained

Cold water

2   cups boiling water

1   package (8-serving size)
    orange flavor gelatin

1½ cups (½ of an 8-ounce
    tub) thawed whipped
    topping

1   can (11 ounces)
    mandarin orange
    segments, drained

1½ cups miniature
    marshmallows

½   cup sweetened flaked
    coconut

According to legend, ambrosia was the food of the gods on Mount Olympus. This dessert is especially enjoyed in the South. Here it is turned into a molded gelatin dessert, which makes it super-easy to serve.

LET'S BEGIN Coat a 6-cup mold with nonstick cooking spray. Drain the pineapple, reserving the juice in a liquid measuring cup. Add enough cold water to measure 1 cup. Stir the boiling water into the gelatin in a large bowl for 2 minutes, or until completely dissolved. Stir in the measured liquid. Refrigerate for 1¼ hours, or until slightly thickened (the consistency of unbeaten egg whites).

STIR IT UP Stir in the whipped topping with a wire whisk until smooth. Refrigerate for 10 minutes or until the mixture will mound.

CHILL & UNMOLD Stir in the remaining ingredients and spoon into the prepared mold. Refrigerate for 3 hours, or until firm. Unmold to serve. Store in the refrigerator.

Makes 10 servings
Per serving: 170 calories, 2g protein, 33g carbohydrates, 4g fat, 4g saturated fat, 0mg cholesterol, 90mg sodium

POPPY SEED FRUIT SALAD

Prep **10 MINUTES + CHILLING**

¼   **cup vegetable oil**

2   **tablespoons lemon juice**

2   **tablespoons honey**

½   **teaspoon poppy seeds**

¼   **teaspoon ground ginger**

¼   **teaspoon ground mustard**

4   **cups assorted cut-up fresh fruit**

Adding poppy seeds to a fruited dressing is a delicious and old-fashioned idea. The combination of lemon and honey, jazzed up with a touch of heat from ground ginger and dry mustard, take this recipe to the next level.

LET'S BEGIN Place the first 6 ingredients in a 1-cup glass measure to make the dressing. Beat with a fork until well combined.

DRESS IT UP Pour the dressing over the fruit in a large salad bowl and toss gently to coat.

CHILL Cover the bowl and refrigerate for at least 1 hour before serving.

Makes 4 servings

Per serving: 238 calories, 2g protein, 30g carbohydrates, 14g fat, 2g saturated fat, 0mg cholesterol, 9mg sodium

---

Food Facts

THE FRUIT SALAD STORY

In the mid-1890s, the Knox Corporation changed the course of salads in America by introducing granulated powdered gelatin, along with a recipe booklet "Dainty Desserts for Dainty People." It went well beyond dessert, including a Jewel Salad of small pineapple and cucumber molds and Luncheon Salad of individual molds of apples, celery, and pecans.

By the turn of the century, the Genesee Pure Food Company purchased the rights (for $450!) for a flavored gelatin dessert product from its creator Pearl Bixby Wait (his wife had named it "Jell-O"). This product turned homemakers all across America who could afford refrigerators into smiling hostesses as they proudly served their latest towering, molded gelatin creation. Though planned as the salad course, folks often saved it for dessert.

Around the 1920s, when electric refrigerators came into vogue, the *frozen* fruit salad began showing up on dinner tables across America. It was an easy-to-fix salad of fruits frozen in a mixture of mayonnaise and whipped cream (see page 112).

ANYTIME FRUIT SALAD

Prep **25 MINUTES + CHILLING**

Lime Dressing (see recipe)

1   tart apple, cut into thin wedges and halved

½   yellow bell pepper, cut into matchstick strips

3   kiwifruit, peeled and sliced

½   cup each halved seedless red and green grapes

½   cup coarsely chopped walnuts

1   cup shredded mild Cheddar cheese (4 ounces)

12   lettuce leaves

The title says it all. This salad is perfect anytime you want a light main course, a first course, or when you just feel a bit hungry. It's just that delicious!

LET'S BEGIN Prepare the Lime Dressing.

DRESS IT UP Combine the next 5 ingredients in a large bowl. Add the dressing and toss.

CHILL & TOSS Cover the bowl and refrigerate for 30 minutes. Add the cheese and toss. Serve on lettuce-lined salad plates.

LIME DRESSING

Blend ¼ cup vegetable oil, 2 tablespoons fresh lime or lemon juice, 2 teaspoons sugar, ¼ teaspoon freshly ground black pepper, and ¼ teaspoon hot-pepper sauce in a small bowl.

Makes 6 servings

Per serving: 249 calories, 6g protein, 9g carbohydrates, 22g fat, 5g saturated fat, 19mg cholesterol, 121mg sodium

FALL FRUIT SALAD

Prep **15 MINUTES + CHILLING**

Yogurt Dressing (see recipe)

2   apples, cored and diced

2   bananas, halved lengthwise, cut into 1-inch pieces

12   dried apricots, quartered

4   pitted prunes, quartered

½   cup golden raisins

The mix of apples, bananas, dried apricots, prunes, and raisins with the sweet yogurt dressing is delicious, but feel free to substitute other favorite fruits, if you like. The yogurt is also fabulous spooned over granola or chunks of cold cooked chicken.

LET'S BEGIN Prepare the Yogurt Dressing.

DRESS IT UP Combine the remaining ingredients in a medium bowl. Gently stir the dressing into the fruit.

CHILL Cover and chill thoroughly, about 1 hour, before serving.

YOGURT DRESSING

Blend ¼ cup plain yogurt or sour cream with 2 tablespoons honey, 1½ tablespoons orange juice (or apple juice, or orange liqueur) and a dash of ground nutmeg to taste in a small bowl.

Makes 6 servings

Per serving: 180 calories, 2g protein, 45g carbohydrates, 0g fat, 0g saturated fat, 1mg cholesterol, 22mg sodium

SUMMERTIME FRUIT SALAD

Prep **20 MINUTES + CHILLING**

½ cup orange juice

¼ cup honey

1 pint strawberries, hulled and halved

½ pint raspberries

½ pint blueberries

2 oranges, peeled and sectioned

1 cup cantaloupe or honeydew melon balls

3 tablespoons fresh mint leaves

The bright and happy fruit flavors of summer come together in this easy and flavorful salad. The easiest way to hull strawberries is with a strawberry huller or with the tip of a paring knife.

LET'S BEGIN In a medium bowl, whisk the juice and honey together until blended.

DRESS IT UP Add the remaining ingredients to the bowl and toss gently to coat well.

CHILL & SERVE Chill for 1 hour. Spoon the salad into 4 individual bowls.

Makes 4 servings

Per serving: 194 calories, 2g protein, 49g carbohydrates, 1g fat, 0g saturated fat, 0mg cholesterol, 8mg sodium

Cook to Cook

HOW DO YOU CHOOSE WHICH FRUITS TO USE IN SALADS?

"*Fruits are a natural in salads*—either in an arranged salad or when tossed in with some greens in the salad bowl. One fruit, such as pink grapefruit slices, is all that's needed with some tender leaf lettuce at the end of a heavy meal. When you want a fruit salad that's something a little more complex and interesting, try tossing together fresh *strawberries, unpeeled red apple slices,*

fresh pear slices, and oranges with a simple vinaigrette made from raspberry vinegar. This combination is a perfect topper spooned over baby greens.

One of my favorite *fruit combos for the holidays* is an arranged salad of a fan of sliced red Bartlett pears (leave the peel on since the color is so nice) and sprinkled with fresh raspberries. Drizzle with mayonnaise thinned

with a little honey and lemon juice. Sprinkle with a few pomegranate seeds.

In summer, I like to toss together *red watermelon balls, chunks of fresh pineapple, fresh strawberry halves, and halved red seedless grapes.* Drizzled with a homemade poppy seed dressing (page 116) and sprinkled with slivered fresh mint leaves, it's pure refreshment."

PEAR & GOAT CHEESE SALAD

Prep **25 MINUTES**   *Cook* **5 MINUTES**

¼ cup walnuts

2 ounces goat cheese or chevre

4 Bartlett or Anjou pears

4 cups mixed salad greens

2 tablespoons balsamic vinegar

1 teaspoon sugar (optional)

1 tablespoon olive oil

Pears have a natural affinity for the flavor of goat cheese. Here pear halves are filled with walnut-coated balls of goat cheese and served over crisp salad greens. Balsamic dressing tops it off and makes it perfect!

LET'S BEGIN Toast the walnuts in a small skillet over medium heat, stirring frequently, for 1 to 5 minutes. Cool a few minutes and finely chop. Cut the cheese into 8 pieces. Shape each into a ball and roll in the walnuts. Set aside.

SCOOP IT OUT Cut the pears in half lengthwise. With a melon baller, remove the seeds and make a small, round cavity in each pear half. Place a cheese ball in each pear cavity. Place ½ cup salad greens on each of 8 plates. Arrange the filled pears on the greens.

DRESS IT UP Pour the vinegar into a small bowl. Add the sugar, if using, whisking until dissolved. Add the oil in a fine stream, whisking constantly, until smooth. Drizzle evenly over pears and sprinkle with any remaining walnuts.

Makes 8 servings

Per serving: 124 calories, 3g protein, 15g carbohydrates, 7g fat, 2g saturated fat, 7mg cholesterol, 32mg sodium

AN ALL-PURPOSE GUIDE TO SALAD-WORTHY FRUITS

Here's your chance to brush up on some tropical, specialty, or more exotic, delicious fruits in the market today. Do you recognize these?

ASIAN PEAR—Has the texture of a pear, the crispness of an apple, and oozes with sweet delicious juice. They vary in size and color, from small and yellow-green to large and golden brown.

BLOOD ORANGE—Looks like any orange, except its rind is smoother and occasionally streaked with red. But that's where the similarity stops. Cut it open and you'll find a bright red flesh that's extra juicy and sweet.

CHARENTAIS MELON—A gem of a melon appearing in some of the gourmet markets these days. It's grayish-green on the outside with dark green stripes, bright orange on the inside, with a scrumptious flowery aroma and a rich honey taste. They're about the size of a small cantaloupe and prized in France and throughout Europe as one of the best!

CRENSHAW MELON—This oval-shaped member of the muskmelon family has a golden-green, smooth, ribbed rind on the outside and a gorgeous orange flesh on the inside. Once you've had a bite of this succulent, luscious melon, you'll know why it's prized as a spectacular choice.

CUSTARD APPLE (Cherimoya)—From the tropics comes this heart-shaped, leathery green fruit with creamy-colored flesh and shiny black seeds. Its flavor is often described as a lovely blend of banana, papaya, and pineapple.

DONUT PEACH—A light yellow, slightly flattened peach with a sunken center, which makes it look like its namesake. The whitish-orange flesh with a heavenly peach flavor makes you very glad you've tried it!

MANGO—We have India to thank for this lovely fruit! It's now grown in the United States and other countries and has become

extremely popular, especially in tropical dishes. Look for an oblong-shaped fruit with a greenish skin that turns yellow as it ripens. It has brilliantly orange flesh with a fragrant taste, plus a large seed. To find out how to cut it easily, turn to page 79.

PAPAYA—It's large, oblong, and yellowish-green and usually hails from either Hawaii or Mexico. Its sunny yellow- to orange-colored flesh is juicy, silky, sweet, and rather exotic in flavor.

POMEGRANATE—Look for a fruit about the size of a large orange with a leathery skin and many seeds hiding in juicy red pulp. These seeds are tiny, edible, and fabulous for garnishing fruit salads.

STARFRUIT (Carambola)—Popular in the Caribbean, Hawaii, and other tropical climates, this fruit is shaped so it looks just like a star when sliced crosswise. Its golden-yellow flesh is fragrant and deliciously juicy.

FRUIT SALAD LANAI

Prep **25 MINUTES**

Chutney Dressing (see recipe)

1   **fresh pineapple**

1   **firm large banana**

1   **orange**

1   **pear**

Mint sprigs

A good trick for removing pineapple flesh from the shell is to use a grapefruit knife. Its serrated edges and curved blade make quick work of this task.

LET'S BEGIN Prepare the Chutney Dressing and set aside.

CUT IT UP Cut the pineapple in half lengthwise through the crown. Cut the pineapple from the shells with a knife leaving the shells intact. Cut the pineapple into chunks.

FILL & SERVE Peel and slice the banana. Peel and section the orange. Core and slice the pear. Place the shells on a serving platter. Mound the fruit in the shells to make pineapple boats. Garnish with mint and serve with the dressing.

CHUTNEY DRESSING

Combine ¼ cup chopped chutney, 3 tablespoons lime juice, 2 tablespoons chopped red bell pepper, 1 tablespoon vegetable oil, 2 teaspoons chopped candied ginger, and ¼ teaspoon curry powder in a covered container. Shake until blended.

> **Makes 6 servings**
> *Per serving: 174 calories, 1g protein, 40g carbohydrates, 3g fat, 0g saturated fat, 0mg cholesterol, 5mg sodium*

Cranberry-Pear Dressing, page 136

Dress It Up!

Many folks pride themselves on making the perfect vinaigrette, then they use it on every salad they toss together. While a basic vinaigrette is an essential task for every cook to master, there are so many more dressings to dress salads with. If you're using strong-flavored greens, such as arugula and radicchio, a full-flavored Balsamic Vinaigrette is the one to whisk together. And when you bring home delicate baby lettuces and mild tender Bibb, whirl up a batch of Classic Honey-Mustard Dressing. Try the Cranberry-Pear Dressing for a lovely mix of fresh citrus and berries or the Smoky Blues Dressing for a bowl of spinach and red onion. The secret is to keep discovering new ways to layer flavors and harmony into the salad bowl with fresh dressings you've made yourself!

SuperQuick
CHERRY-WALNUT VINAIGRETTE

Prep **5 MINUTES**

¼ cup dried tart cherries (1½ ounces)

1 small to medium shallot

2 garlic cloves, peeled

¾ cup fruit-flavored vinegar

6 tablespoons orange juice

3 tablespoons honey

1½ cups walnut oil

Salt and freshly ground black pepper (optional)

We know you will find lots of tasty ways to use this fabulous vinaigrette, such as drizzling it over mixed greens, poached salmon, grilled boneless chicken breasts, or leftover rice for a great salad.

LET'S BEGIN Place the cherries, shallot, and garlic in a food processor and pulse until they are finely chopped.

PUREE IT FAST Add the fruit-flavored vinegar, orange juice, and honey to the processor and purée the mixture.

BLEND & TASTE Then, with the food processor on, slowly add the walnut oil through the feed tube, processing until well combined. Add salt and pepper to taste, if you wish.

Makes 3 cups

Per serving (2 tablespoons each): 140 calories, 0g protein, 5g carbohydrates, 14g fat, 1g saturated fat, 0mg cholesterol, 1mg sodium

SuperQuick

RASPBERRY ZINGER VINAIGRETTE

Prep **22 MINUTES**

2 **Raspberry Zinger tea bags**

½ **cup distilled white vinegar**

¾ **cup olive oil**

1 **teaspoon balsamic vinegar**

1 **teaspoon sugar**

Raspberry Zinger tea, which has been popular for many years, makes a surprisingly tasty addition to basic vinaigrette. For the white vinegar, you can use white wine vinegar or distilled white vinegar.

LET'S BEGIN Place the tea bags and vinegar in a jar. Let the tea bags steep for 20 minutes. Remove the bags and gently squeeze the last bit of liquid from them before discarding.

SHAKE IT UP Add the remaining ingredients to the vinegar. Cover the jar tightly and shake until well blended.

Makes 1¼ cups

Per serving (2 tablespoons each): 147 calories, 0g protein, 1g carbohydrates, 16g fat, 2g saturated fat, 0mg cholesterol, 1mg sodium

---

Salad Basics

VINAIGRETTES 101

To put it as simply as possible, a vinaigrette is a combination of oil and vinegar. It can be temporary vinaigrette, which is achieved by whisking, blending, or shaking the liquids together until they're suspended (emulsified) into a dressing, but after a few minutes they'll separate again. Or it can be a stable vinaigrette, which is held together (emulsified) with Dijon mustard or another emulsifier such as a fruit or vegetable purée (such as roasted red pepper purée). This type can be stored in the refrigerator, as it stays "together" without separating.

The key to a perfectly stable vinaigrette is using the proper proportion of oil to vinegar: the rule of thumb is 1 part vinegar (or other acid such as lemon juice) to 3 to 4 parts oil. As for the mustard, begin with a nice dollop.

THE ACID Whether you use red wine vinegar, apple cider vinegar, fresh lemon juice, sherry vinegar, or a combination is a matter of personal choice. If you are not sure which you prefer, go with the classic choice—red wine vinegar, preferably one that is of good quality.

THE OIL Here, too, the oil you choose is a matter of personal preference. Use an extra-virgin olive oil—any supermarket available brand will do—or if you prefer a lighter oil flavor, go with canola oil or a combination of both olive and canola oils.

THE TECHNIQUE Combine the mustard and vinegar in a bowl (glass is best because it won't wobble) and whisk them together until nice and smooth. Very slowly add the oil, at first a couple of drops at a time, whisking all the while so the mixture remains thick and smooth. After adding about one-third of the oil, you can add the remaining oil in a thin, steady stream. Then add salt and freshly ground black pepper to taste, check to see if more mustard is needed, and you're done!

SuperQuick
TARRAGON VINAIGRETTE

Prep **5 MINUTES**

¼ cup canola oil

2 tablespoons tarragon vinegar

1 teaspoon Dijon mustard

½ teaspoon celery salt

1 garlic clove, crushed

Freshly ground black pepper (optional)

Serve this full-flavored vinaigrette over your favorite green salad or one made of lettuce, endive, celery, and green bell pepper.

WHISK IT FAST Whisk together the first 5 ingredients in a small bowl. Add the pepper to taste, if you wish.

Makes ⅓ cup

Per serving (2 tablespoons each): 184 calories, 0g protein, 1g carbohydrates, 20g fat, 1g saturated fat, 0mg cholesterol, 225mg sodium

SuperQuick
SPRING VANILLA VINAIGRETTE

Prep **5 MINUTES**

⅓ cup olive oil

3 tablespoons white wine vinegar

1 teaspoon vanilla extract

1 teaspoon dried tarragon leaves

¼ teaspoon freshly ground black pepper

½ teaspoon sugar

½ teaspoon salt

The unusual combination of vanilla and tarragon makes this dressing quite fabulous. Mix it with a simple green salad, lobster salad, or chicken salad.

WHISK IT FAST Whisk together all of the ingredients in a small bowl until well blended. Chill before tossing with salad, if you wish.

Makes 4 servings

Per serving (2 tablespoons each): 166 calories, 0g protein, 1g carbohydrates, 18g fat, 2g saturated fat, 0mg cholesterol, 294mg sodium

Spring Vanilla Vinaigrette

SuperQuick
BALSAMIC VINAIGRETTE

Prep **10 MINUTES**

3   tablespoons olive oil

¼   cup balsamic vinegar

2   teaspoons Dijon-style
      mustard

3   tablespoons chicken
      broth

¾   teaspoon sugar

¼   teaspoon salt

¼   teaspoon freshly ground
      black pepper

1   tablespoon chopped
      fresh basil leaves
      (optional)

For the most flavor here, buy the best balsamic vinegar your wallet can handle in a specialty food store or Italian grocery.

WHISK IT FAST Combine all of the ingredients except the basil in a medium bowl and whisk until well blended. Add the chopped fresh basil before serving, if you wish.

Makes ¾ cup

Per serving (2 tablespoons each): 71 calories, 0g protein, 2g carbohydrates, 7g fat, 1g saturated fat, 0mg cholesterol, 168mg sodium

---

Food Facts

THE LATEST NEWS ABOUT BALSAMIC VINEGARS

This thick and lustrous vinegar—with the rich color of mahogany—is the finest vinegar in the world! It is crafted in the Emilia-Romagna region of northern Italy and is famed for its unsurpassed flavor and high cost.

Authentic balsamic (there are many imitators on the market) is made by allowing freshly crushed grape juice (known as *must*) to ferment into wine. It is then simmered to concentrate its flavor and finally allowed to very slowly ferment for several years so its sugar turns into acetic acid (vinegar). Lastly, it is aged for decades—or even centuries—in a series of increasingly smaller barrels, where it continues to reduce and condense. The barrels are often made of oak, the preferred wood for the process.

To be labeled Aceto Balsamico Tradizionale (and very few of the vinegars are), the vinegar must be aged for a minimum of 12 years. Because of the concentrated flavor, this liquid jewel is used in very small amounts.

ROASTED TOMATO VINAIGRETTE

Prep **15 MINUTES** *Grill* **10 MINUTES + COOLING**

Roasted Plum Tomato (see recipe)

½ teaspoon ground cumin

Pinch of cayenne

¼ teaspoon salt

¼ teaspoon freshly ground black pepper

½ cup canola oil

¼ cup balsamic vinegar, or 2 tablespoons lemon juice + 2 tablespoons balsamic vinegar

Roasting a meaty plum tomato makes a special addition to a simple vinaigrette. Drizzle it over sliced grilled steak, sautéed shrimp, or steamed green beans.

LET'S BEGIN Prepare one Roasted Plum Tomato and put in a medium bowl.

WHISK IT FAST Add the cumin, cayenne, salt, and pepper to the pulp in a medium bowl and mash together with the back of a spoon to make a paste. Whisk in the oil and vinegar until well blended.

ROASTED PLUM TOMATO

Cut 1 plum tomato in half and rub with ½ teaspoon olive oil and sprinkle with salt and freshly ground black pepper. Grill over low heat for 10 to 12 minutes turning once. Let cool slightly, about 10 minutes. Peel the blackened skin off the tomato and squeeze out the seeds and discard. There should be about 1 tablespoon pulp remaining.

Makes about ¾ cup

Per serving (2 tablespoons each): 175 calories, 0g protein, 2g carbohydrates, 19g fat, 1g saturated fat, 0mg cholesterol, 98mg sodium

DOUBLE FRUIT DRESSING

Prep **10 MINUTES**

¼   cup vegetable oil

¼   cup Concord grape juice

2   tablespoons lemon juice

½   teaspoon grated lemon zest

½   teaspoon chopped fresh mint leaves

1   teaspoon peeled grated fresh ginger (optional)

Salt (optional)

Bet you thought grape juice was just for drinking. Dress whichever mixed greens and salad toppings you like with this tangy dressing. It goes great on fruit salads too. Whisk up the dressing from grape juice, then spark it with fresh lemon.

WHISK IT FAST Whisk the first 5 ingredients together in a small bowl. Add ginger and salt, if you wish.

Makes ¾ cup

Per serving (2 tablespoons each): 88 calories, 0g protein, 2g carbohydrates, 9g fat, 1g saturated fat, 0mg cholesterol, 0mg sodium

Time Savers

A FAST FLAVOR BOOST FOR PACKAGED CROUTONS

Supermarket croutons are a great pantry item to keep on hand. You can use them to spark up many different dishes: Top a simple green salad with a handful, crush them and use to coat boneless chicken breasts, or sprinkle them over a favorite casserole. So stock up on the plain variety and try one of these ideas:

- Melt 1 stick butter, toss in 1 minced large garlic clove, and cook until golden. Add the croutons and toss. Immediately sprinkle with Italian herb seasoning to coat.
- Coat plain croutons with cooking spray and toss the croutons with packaged grated Parmesan until coated.
- Toss the croutons in warm olive oil, then in a blend of chili powder, dried oregano, salt, freshly ground black pepper, and cayenne.
- Toss the croutons in heated olive oil, then into Cajun seasoning.

Tip: Put croutons into a resealable bag with the seasoning. Seal and shake until evenly coated. If the croutons are warm, wait a few minutes before tossing.

CLASSIC HONEY-MUSTARD DRESSING

Prep **5 MINUTES**

The calorie count of this dressing is great. If you are not watching your calories, however, you can substitute reduced-fat or regular mayonnaise.

1¼	cups nonfat mayonnaise
⅓	cup honey
1	tablespoon vinegar
⅔	cup vegetable oil
1	teaspoon dried onion flakes
2	tablespoons chopped fresh parsley
2	tablespoons Dijon or regular mustard

WHISK IT FAST Whisk together all ingredients in a small bowl until well blended. Cover and refrigerate until ready to serve.

Makes 2½ cups

Per serving (2 tablespoons each): 93 calories, 0g protein, 7g carbohydrates, 7g fat, 1g saturated fat, 0mg cholesterol, 137mg sodium

---

Cook to Cook

WHAT SALADS PAIR WELL WITH HONEY-MUSTARD DRESSING?

❝Whirl up the recipe for Classic Honey-Mustard Dressing and drizzle it on one of these suggestions. They match with the dressing perfectly.

- Broccoli Slaw: Honey-mustard dressing stands up well to the big flavor of broccoli slaw. I like to add some julienned apple to the mix as well.

- Chopped Salad: **When I dress chopped salad with honey-mustard,** I like to add some chopped pears and raisins along with the ham, cheese, carrots, celery, and scallions that I usually include.

- Sliced Red and Yellow Tomatoes: I was surprised by the way the **honey-mustard dressing brings out the sweetness of tomatoes.**

- Smoked Chicken or Turkey Salad: This is one of our favorites. Chunks of already cooked smoked chicken or turkey tossed with sliced carrots, coarsely chopped green bell pepper, and **the honey-mustard dressing makes a quick busy-night main dish salad.**❞

COOKED CREAMY CAESAR DRESSING

Prep **5 MINUTES + CHILLING**   *Cook* **2 MINUTES**

½	cup vegetable oil
1	garlic clove, crushed
2	large egg yolks
2	tablespoons red wine vinegar
2	tablespoons lemon juice
¼	teaspoon mustard powder
⅛	teaspoon Worcestershire sauce

Here's how to make a fabulous Caesar salad. Buy a package of baby romaine hearts, separate and wash the leaves well, then spin them dry. Put the whole leaves into your favorite wooden salad bowl, top with packaged croutons and lots of grated Parmesan, and finish off with this very excellent dressing.

LET'S BEGIN Combine the oil and garlic in a jar with a tight-fitting lid. Refrigerate the mixture 2 hours or overnight. To use, remove and discard the garlic. Set the oil aside.

COOK IT LOW Combine the remaining ingredients and cook in a small saucepan over very low heat, stirring constantly, for about 2 minutes, or until the mixture thickens and bubbles at the edges. Remove from the heat. Let stand to cool for about 5 minutes.

SHAKE IT UP Add the egg mixture to the oil in the jar, cover, and shake until well blended. Chill if not using immediately.

> *Makes ⅔ cup*
> *Per serving (2 tablespoons each): 190 calories, 1g protein, 1g carbohydrates, 21g fat, 3g saturated fat, 72mg cholesterol, 4mg sodium*

SuperQuick
RANCH SALAD DRESSING

Prep **5 MINUTES**

Powdered coffee creamer makes everyone's favorite dressing even more tempting. Be sure to whisk or shake it well before using.

¾   **cup water**

⅓   **cup powdered coffee creamer**

1   **packet (1 ounce) ranch salad dressing mix**

1   **cup mayonnaise**

LET'S BEGIN Whisk together the water and coffee creamer in a medium bowl until smooth.

MIX IT UP Whisk in the dressing mix and mayonnaise. Store covered in the refrigerator for up to 1 week.

Makes 2 cups

Per serving (2 tablespoons each): 147 calories, 0g protein, 6g carbohydrates, 5g fat, 1g saturated fat, 4mg cholesterol, 495mg sodium

---

Salad Basics

4 EASY WAYS TO FLAVOR RANCH DRESSING

Whirl up some of our Ranch Salad Dressing and try on one of these salads . . . they're winners!

- **RIVIERA RANCH:** Create a main-dish salad of blanched green beans, sliced cooked new potatoes, sliced hard-cooked eggs, and grilled fresh tuna or canned tuna. Add some chopped fresh or crumbled dried rosemary and lots of chopped Niçoise olives. Toss with the Ranch Salad Dressing.

- **RODEO RANCH:** Mix iceberg and Romaine lettuces together with ripe tomato wedges. Stir a chopped chipotle into the Ranch Salad Dressing, then toss with the salad.

- **ROMAN RANCH:** Make a salad of arugula, Italian tomatoes, and roasted bell peppers. Then stir a little Italian dry seasoning and Parmesan cheese into the Ranch Salad Dressing and toss on the salad.

- **RHINELAND RANCH:** Stir in some brown mustard and caraway seeds to the Ranch Salad Dressing and use to dress your next potato salad.

CRANBERRY-PEAR DRESSING
Prep **7 MINUTES**

1	cup jellied cranberry sauce
½	cup diced canned pears
½	cup pear syrup, reserved
⅛	teaspoon ground ginger

Three ingredients are turned into an especially delicious, creamy dressing that is perfect for serving with leftover Thanksgiving turkey, deli-roasted chicken, or thick slices of ham.

PROCESS IT FAST Place all of the ingredients in a food processor. Process on high for 2 minutes, or until the mixture is smooth.

Makes 2 cups

Per serving (2 tablespoons each): 30 calories, 0g protein, 8g carbohydrates, 0g fat, 0g saturated fat, 0mg cholesterol, 4mg sodium

PARMESAN-CURRY DRESSING
Prep **10 MINUTES**

½	cup nonfat plain yogurt
½	cup buttermilk
1½	teaspoons sugar
1	tablespoon grated Parmesan cheese
¼	teaspoon freshly ground black pepper
⅛	teaspoon onion powder
1	teaspoon drained capers
⅛	teaspoon curry powder

If curry is a spice you love, prepare the recipe as is, then add more curry powder to suit your taste. The dressing is ideal for spooning over sliced tomatoes, a crisp green salad, or cold sliced chicken or turkey.

PROCESS IT FAST In a blender or food processor, blend all of the ingredients well.

Makes 1 cup

Per serving (2 tablespoons each): 21 calories, 2g protein, 3g carbohydrates, 0g fat, 0g saturated fat, 1mg cholesterol, 48mg sodium

Cranberry-Pear Dressing

SMOKY BLUES DRESSING

Prep **10 MINUTES + CHILLING**

½   cup smoked almonds

1   cup evaporated milk

1   cup mayonnaise

1   cup plain yogurt

1   cup blue cheese or
     Gorgonzola, softened
     (4 ounces)

1   tablespoon apple cider
     vinegar

⅛   teaspoon freshly ground
     black pepper

Spoon this delectably creamy dressing over sliced grilled chicken or a romaine and tomato salad.

LET'S BEGIN Place the almonds in a food processor. Cover and process until almonds are coarsely chopped.

MIX & CHILL Combine the chopped almonds with the remaining ingredients in a medium bowl. Cover and refrigerate for 2 hours before serving.

Makes about 3½ cups

Per serving (2 tablespoons): 80 calories, 2g protein, 4g carbohydrates, 6g fat, 2g saturated fat, 9mg cholesterol, 152mg sodium

ZESTY DIJONNAISE BLUE CHEESE DRESSING

Prep **5 MINUTES**

½ cup creamy Dijon
    mustard and mayonnaise
    blend

¼ cup prepared chunky
    blue cheese dressing

2 tablespoons milk
   (optional)

Use this dressing as a dipping sauce for a variety of raw vegetables or even potato chips or serve it over salad greens.

FIX IT FAST Blend all the ingredients in a small bowl, adding milk if you wish for the desired consistency.

Makes ¾ cup

Per serving (2 tablespoons each): 71 calories, 0g protein, 5g carbohydrates, 5g fat, 1g saturated fat, 2mg cholesterol, 392mg sodium

---

Salad Basics

THE BLUES OF BLUE CHEESE

Blue cheeses are made in almost every country in the cheese-making areas of the world: Denmark, England, France, and America. They vary in fat content, craftsmanship, and aging time—and in the mold that creates their flavor, prestige, and cost. There are many to choose from, but here are a few international classics you might want to look for:

- **ROQUEFORT:** An unpasteurized French cheese made from sheep's milk, it is crumbly and salty with a blue-green interior mold.

- **GORGONZOLA:** An Italian pasteurized cow's milk cheese, it is creamy and sweet in flavor with a hint of spice.

- **STILTON:** England's traditional pasteurized cow's milk blue cheese has blue-green veining and a rich, spicy flavor.

- **DANISH BLUE:** A mass-market cow's milk cheese, Danish Blue (Danablu) is flavorful, creamy in texture, and easy to handle. It is an affordable choice for dressings, dips, spreads, and salads.

- **MAYTAG BLUE:** Made in Iowa since 1941, this unpasteurized cow's milk cheese was one of the first new-wave artisan cheeses in America.

Tip: Pick one from the list and crumble it on a fresh spinach salad with fresh pears and red onion and tossed with a balsamic vinaigrette . . . delicious!

CREDITS

PAGE 2 Dole: Photo for Tomato, Prosciutto & Fresh Mozzarella courtesy of the Dole Food Company. Used with permission.

PAGE 8 Kraft Foods: Photo for Classic California Cobb courtesy of Kraft Kitchens. Used with permission.

PAGE 16 Sargento: Photo for Fruit & Cheese Salad courtesy of Sargento Food Inc. Used with permission.

PAGE 18 National Honey Board: Recipe for Almond Lettuce Wedges with Honey Mustard courtesy of the National Honey Board. Used with permission.

PAGE 19 Ocean Spray Cranberries: Photo and recipe for Cranberry Spinach Salad with Dijon Bacon Dressing courtesy of Ocean Spray Cranberries, Inc. Used with permission.

PAGES 20/21 Dole: Photo and recipe for Americana Salad courtesy of the Dole Food Company. Used with permission.

PAGE 22 Canolainfo: Recipe for Spinach Salad with Citrus Vinaigrette courtesy of Canolainfo. Used with permission.

PAGE 23 Cherry Marketing Institute: Photo and recipe for Asian Spinach Salad courtesy of The Cherry Marketing Institute. Used with permission.

PAGE 24 Dole: Photo and recipe for Springtime Spinach Salad courtesy of Dole Food Company. Used with permission.

PAGE 25 Dole: Photo and recipe for California Classic Salad with Roquefort courtesy of Dole Food Company. Used with permission.

PAGES 26/27 Sargento: Photo and recipe for Quick Caesar Salad courtesy of Sargento Foods Inc. Used with permission.

PAGE 28 National Pork Board: Recipe for Beet, Walnut & Blue Cheese courtesy of the National Pork Board. Used with permission.

PAGE 29 Produce for Better Health Foundation: Photo and recipe for Avocado Garden Salad courtesy of the Produce for Better Health Foundation. Used with permission.

PAGES 30/31 Dole: Photo and recipe for Tomato, Prosciutto & Fresh Mozzarella courtesy of Dole Food Company. Used with permission.

PAGE 30 Earthbound Farm: Recipe for Mixed Baby Greens with Apple, Bacon & Stilton courtesy of Earthbound Farm. Used with permission.

PAGE 32 Earthbound Farm: Photo and recipe for Golden Gate Salad courtesy of Earthbound Farm. Used with permission.

PAGE 33 Florida Tomato Committee: Recipe for Marinated Goat Cheese & Tomato Salad courtesy of Florida Tomato Committee. Used with permission.

PAGE 34 Ocean Spray Cranberries: Recipe for Quick Mandarin-Cranberry Salad courtesy of Ocean Spray Cranberries, Inc. Used with permission.

PAGE 35 California Strawberry Commission: Photo and recipe for Strawberry & Stilton on Mixed Greens courtesy of the © California Strawberry Commission. All rights reserved. Used with permission.

PAGES 36/37 National Pork Board: Photo and recipe for BLT Salad courtesy of the National Pork Board. Used with permission.

PAGE 37 Sunkist: Recipe for Green & Orange with Blue Cheese courtesy of Sunkist Growers, Inc. Used with permission.

PAGE 38 Land O'Lakes: Recipe for Pear & Walnut Salad with Blue Cheese courtesy of Land O'Lakes, Inc. Used with permission.

PAGE 38 Sargento: Recipe for Fruit & Cheese Salad courtesy of Sargento Food Inc. Used with permission.

PAGE 39 Wish-Bone: Recipe for Antipasto Salad courtesy of Wish-Bone®. Used with permission.

PAGE 40 Sargento: Photo for Perfect Pasta Salad Toss courtesy of Sargento Foods Inc. Used with permission.

PAGE 42 Cattlemen's Beef Board: Photo and recipe for Beef, Pasta & Artichoke Salad courtesy of Cattlemen's Beef Board and National Cattlemen's Beef Association. Used with permission.

PAGE 43 French's: Recipe for Grilled London Broil Salad courtesy of French's® Honey Dijon Mustard. Used with permission.

PAGE 44 Sargento: Photo and recipe for Easy Taco Salad courtesy of Sargento Foods Inc. Used with permission.

PAGE 45 Sargento: Photo and recipe for Classic Chef Salad courtesy of Sargento Foods Inc. Used with permission.

PAGES 46/47 French's: Photo and recipe for Citrus Pork Tenderloin & Spinach Salad courtesy of French's® French Fried Onions. Used with permission.

PAGE 48 Wish-Bone: Recipe for Deluxe Chef's Salad courtesy of Wish-Bone®. Used with permission.

PAGE 48 Dole: Recipe for BLT Salad with Bow Ties courtesy of Dole Food Company. Used with permission.

PAGE 49 Kraft Foods: Photo and recipe for Tangy Tuna Macaroni Salad courtesy of Kraft Kitchens. Used with permission.

PAGE 50 Wish-Bone: Recipe for Caramelized Apple Salad with Grilled Chicken courtesy of Wish-Bone®. Used with permission.

PAGE 51 National Chicken Council: Photo and recipe for California Chicken Salad courtesy of the National Chicken Council/U.S. Poultry & Egg Association. Used with permission.

PAGE 52 National Honey Board: Photo and recipe for Farmers' Market Chicken Salad courtesy of the National Honey Board. Used with permission.

PAGE 53 National Honey Board: Photo and recipe for Waldorf Chicken Salad courtesy of the National Honey Board. Used with permission.

PAGES 54/55 Kraft Foods: Photo and recipe for Classic California Cobb courtesy of Kraft Kitchens. Used with permission.

PAGE 56 Cherry Marketing Institute: Photo and recipe for Chicken & Wild Rice Salad courtesy of The Cherry Marketing Institute. Used with permission.

PAGE 57 Cherry Marketing Institute: Photo and recipe for Shrimp Salad with Dried Cherries courtesy of The Cherry Marketing Institute. Used with permission.

PAGE 58 Bumble Bee: Recipe for Tuna Salad Elegante courtesy of Bumble Bee Seafoods. Used with permission.

PAGE 59 McCormick: Recipe for Tasty Tuna Salad courtesy of McCormick. Used with permission.

PAGES 60/61 Ocean Spray Cranberries: Photo and recipe for Seafood Salad with White Grapefruit Vinaigrette courtesy of Ocean Spray Cranberries, Inc. Used with permission.

PAGE 62 Association of Dressings & Sauces: Recipe for Catalina Seafood Salad courtesy of The Association of Dressings & Sauces. Used with permission.

PAGE 63 American Egg Board: Recipe for Salade à la Niçoise courtesy of the American Egg Board. Used with permission.

PAGE 64 Kraft Foods: Recipe for Egg Salad courtesy of Kraft Kitchens. Used with permission.

PAGE 64 Sargento: Recipe for California Chopped Salad courtesy of Sargento Foods Inc. Used with permission.

PAGE 65 Sargento: Recipe for Perfect Pasta Salad Toss courtesy of Sargento Foods Inc. Used with permission.

PAGE 66 Sargento: Photo for Mexican Chopped Salad courtesy of Sargento Foods Inc. Used with permission.

PAGE 68 Sargento: Photo and recipe for Mexican Cobb Salad courtesy of Sargento Foods Inc. Used with permission.

PAGE 69 French's: Recipe for Thai Beef Salad courtesy of French's® Worcestershire Sauce and Frank's® RedHot® Cayenne Pepper Sauce. Used with permission.

PAGES 70/71 Cattlemen's Beef Board: Photo and recipe for Greek Beef Salad courtesy of Cattlemen's Beef Board and National Cattlemen's Beef Association. Used with permission.

PAGE 72 Canolainfo: Recipe for Layered Mexican Salad courtesy of Canolainfo. Used with permission.

PAGE 73 National Honey Board: Photo and recipe for South of the Border Salad with Honey-Jalapeño Dressing courtesy of the National Honey Board. Used with permission.

PAGE 74 National Chicken Council: Recipe for Curried Chicken & Spinach Salad courtesy of the National Chicken Council/U.S. Poultry and Egg Association. Used with permission.

PAGE 75 French's: Recipe for Spicy Thai Shrimp Salad courtesy of Frank's® RedHot® Cayenne Pepper Sauce. Used with permission.

PAGE 76 Bumble Bee: Recipe for Mediterranean Tuna Salad with Pancetta Vinaigrette courtesy of Bumble Bee Seafoods. Used with permission.

PAGE 77 Wish-Bone: Recipe for Mediterranean Tomato Salad courtesy of Wish-Bone®. Used with permission.

PAGE 78 Sargento: Photo and recipe for Mexican Chopped Salad courtesy of Sargento Foods Inc. Used with permission.

PAGE 79 California Strawberry Commission: Recipe for Island Mango-Berry Salad courtesy of © California Strawberry Commission. All rights reserved. Used with permission.

PAGE 80 McCormick: Photo for Old Bay Coleslaw courtesy of McCormick. Used with permission.

PAGE 82 Tone Brothers: Photo and recipe for Green Bean Salad courtesy of Tone Brothers, Inc., producer of Tone's, Spice Islands, and Durkee products. Used with permission.

PAGE 83 Zatarain's: Recipe for Four Bean Salad courtesy of Zatarain's. Used with permission.

PAGE 84 Land O'Lakes: Photo and recipe for Cajun Black-Eyed Pea & Pimento Salad courtesy of Land O'Lakes, Inc. Used with permission.

PAGE 85 Tone Brothers: Recipe for Fiesta Corn Salad courtesy of Tone Brothers, Inc., producer of Tone's, Spice Islands, and Durkee products. Used with permission.

PAGE 85 National Pork Board: Recipe for Cool Cucumber Salad courtesy of the National Pork Board. Used with permission.

PAGES 86/87 Ocean Spray Cranberries: Photo and recipe for Crimson Slaw courtesy of Ocean Spray Cranberries, Inc. Used with permission.

PAGE 88 Domino: Recipe for Country Coleslaw courtesy of Domino Sugar. Used with permission.

PAGE 89 McCormick: Photo and recipe for Old Bay Coleslaw courtesy of McCormick. Used with permission.

PAGE 90 Produce for Better Health Foundation: Recipe for Warm Red Cabbage & Bacon courtesy of the Produce for Better Health Foundation. Used with permission.

PAGE 91 National Honey Board: Recipe for Red-Skin Potato Salad with Honey Dill Dressing courtesy of National Honey Board. Used with permission.

PAGE 92 United States Potato Board: Recipe for French Potato Salad courtesy of United States Potato Board. Used with permission.

PAGE 93 United States Potato Board: Recipe for All-American Potato Salad courtesy of United States Potato Board. Used with permission.

PAGES 94/95 Land O'Lakes: Photo and recipe for Easy Hot German Potato Salad courtesy of Land O'Lakes, Inc. Used with permission.

PAGES 96 Land O'Lakes: Photo and recipe for Sour Cream Dill Potato Salad courtesy of Land O'Lakes, Inc. Used with permission.

WEB SITES

PAGES 97 Domino: Recipe for Country Macaroni Salad courtesy of Domino Sugar. Used with permission.

PAGES 98/99 Canolainfo: Photo and recipe for Pasta Salad courtesy of Canolainfo. Used with permission.

PAGE 100 Land O'Lakes: Photo and recipe for Zesty Summer Pasta Salad courtesy of Land O'Lakes, Inc. Used with permission.

PAGE 101 Uncle Ben's: Photo and recipe for Carrot Raisin Rice Salad courtesy of UNCLE BEN'S® Brand. Used with permission.

PAGES 102/103 Florida Tomato Committee: Photo and recipe for Tomato & Bulgur Salad courtesy of the Florida Tomato Committee. Used with permission.

PAGE 104 Dole: Photo and recipe for Moroccan Fruit Salad courtesy of Dole Food Company. Used with permission.

PAGE 105 Sargento: Photo and recipe for Market Salad courtesy of Sargento Foods Inc. Used with permission.

PAGE 106 Kraft Foods: Photo for Fresh Fruit Parfait Mold courtesy of Kraft Kitchens. Used with permission.

PAGE 108 Ocean Spray Cranberries: Photo and recipe for Light & Fruity Raspberry Mold courtesy of Ocean Spray Cranberries, Inc. Used with permission.

PAGE 109 Kraft Foods: Recipe for Layered Orange Pineapple Mold courtesy of Kraft Kitchens. Used with permission.

PAGE 110 Kraft Foods: Photo and recipe for Fresh Fruit Parfait Mold courtesy of Kraft Kitchens. Used with permission.

PAGE 111 Kraft Foods: Recipe for Creamy Fruited Mold courtesy of Kraft Kitchens. Used with permission.

PAGE 112 Dole: Recipe for Grandma's Frozen Salad courtesy of the Dole Food Company. Used with permission.

PAGE 113 National Honey Board: Recipe for Ambrosia with Honey Lime Cream courtesy of the National Honey Board. Used with permission.

PAGES 114/115 Kraft Foods: Photo and recipe for Ambrosia Mold courtesy of Kraft Kitchens. Used with permission.

PAGE 116 McCormick: Recipe for Poppy Seed Fruit Salad courtesy of McCormick. Used with permission.

PAGE 117 Sargento: Photo and recipe for Anytime Fruit Salad courtesy of Sargento Foods Inc. Used with permission.

PAGE 118 National Honey Board: Recipe for Fall Fruit Salad courtesy of the National Honey Board. Used with permission.

PAGE 119 California Strawberry Commission: Recipe for Summertime Fruit Salad courtesy of © California Strawberry Commission. All rights reserved. Used with permission.

PAGES 120/121 California Walnut Marketing Board: Photo and recipe for Pear & Goat Cheese Salad courtesy of the California Walnut Marketing Board. Used with permission.

PAGE 123 Dole: Recipe for Fruit Salad Lanai courtesy of Dole Food Company. Used with permission.

PAGE 124 Ocean Spray Cranberries: Photo for Cranberry-Pear Dressing courtesy of Ocean Spray Cranberries, Inc. Used with permission.

PAGE 126 Cherry Marketing Institute: Photo and recipe for Cherry-Walnut Vinaigrette courtesy of The Cherry Marketing Institute. Used with permission.

PAGE 127 Celestial Seasonings: Recipe for Raspberry Zinger Vinaigrette courtesy of Celestial Seasonings. Used with permission.

PAGE 128 Canolainfo: Recipe for Tarragon Vinaigrette courtesy of Canolainfo. Used with permission.

PAGES 128/129 McCormick: Recipe for Spring Vanilla Vinaigrette courtesy of McCormick. Used with permission.

PAGE 130 Nestlé: Recipe for Balsamic Vinaigrette courtesy of Nestlé. Used with permission.

PAGE 131 Canolainfo: Recipe for Roasted Tomato Vinaigrette courtesy of Canolainfo. Used with permission.

PAGE 132 Welch's: Recipe for Double Fruit Dressing courtesy of the Welch's, the New York Wine & Grape Foundation, and the National Grape Cooperative. Used with permission.

PAGE 133 National Honey Board: Recipe for Classic Honey-Mustard Dressing courtesy of the National Honey Board. Used with permission.

PAGE 134 American Egg Board: Recipe for Cooked Creamy Caesar Dressing courtesy of the American Egg Board. Used with permission.

PAGE 135 Nestlé: Recipe for Ranch Salad Dressing courtesy of Nestlé. Used with permission.

PAGE 136 The Sugar Association: Recipe for Parmesan-Curry Dressing courtesy of The Sugar Association. Used with permission.

PAGES 136/137 Ocean Spray Cranberries: Photo and recipe for Cranberry-Pear Dressing courtesy of Ocean Spray Cranberries, Inc. Used with permission.

PAGE 138 Nestlé: Recipe for Smoky Blues Dressing courtesy of Nestlé. Used with permission.

PAGE 139 Wish-Bone: Recipe for Zesty Dijonnaise Blue Cheese Dressing courtesy of Wish-Bone®. Used with permission.

RODALE INC.
www.rodale.com

American Egg Board
www.aeb.org

Association of Dressings and Sauces
www.dressings-sauces.org

Bumble Bee
www.bumblebee.com

California Strawberry Commission
www.calstrawberry.com

California Walnut Marketing Board
www.walnuts.org

Canolainfo
www.canolainfo.org

Cattlemen's Beef Board
www.beefitswhatsfordinner.com

Celestial Seasonings
www.celestialseasonings.com

Cherry Marketing Institute
www.usacherries.com

Dole Food Company
www.dole.com

Domino
www.dominosugar.com

Earthbound Farm
www.earthboundfarm.com

Florida Tomato Committee
www.floridatomatoes.org

French's
www.frenchsfoods.com

Kraft Foods
www.kraftfoods.com

Land O'Lakes
www.landolakes.com

McCormick
www.mccormick.com

National Chicken Council
www.eatchicken.com

National Honey Board
www.honey.com

National Pork Board
www.otherwhitemeat.com

Nestlé
www.meals.com

Ocean Spray Cranberries
www.oceanspray.com

Produce for Better Health Foundation
www.5aday.org

Sargento
www.sargentocheese.com

The Sugar Association
www.sugar.org

Sunkist
www.sunkist.com

Tone Brothers
www.spiceadvice.com

Uncle Ben's
www.unclebens.com

United States Potato Board
www.potatohelp.com

Welch's
www.welchs.com

Wish-Bone
www.wish-bone.com

Zatarain's
www.zatarain.com

INDEX

✔ Designates a SuperQuick recipe that gets you in and out of the kitchen in 30 minutes or less! **Boldface** page numbers refer to photographs. *Italicized* page numbers refer to boxed text.